The Natural Foods

HEALTHY BABY COOKBOOK

DELICIOUS WHOLEFOOD RECIPES FOR BABIES AND CHILDREN

by

CAROL HUNTER

Illustrated by Paul Davies

THORSONS PUBLISHING GROUP
Wellingborough, Northamptonshire
·
Rochester, Vermont

First published 1985
Second Impression 1986
Third Impression 1987

British Library Cataloguing in Publication Data

Hunter, Carol
   The natural foods healthy baby cookbook.
   1. Cookery (Natural foods)   2. Children —
   Nutrition
   I. Title
   641.5'637   TX652

ISBN 0-7225-0837-9

Printed in Great Britain by
Richard Clay (The Chaucer Press) Ltd,
Bungay, Suffolk

CONTENTS

INTRODUCTION

When I first started planning this book, I had ambitious ideas about elaborate recipes from which a doting mother could prepare gourmet meals for her baby. It was only when I started the actual research, while at the same time weaning my third child, that I realized I was on completely the wrong tack.

If you are preparing babyfoods at home, the emphasis *must* be on speed, simplicity and convenience; and the way to fulfil these criteria is to rely on fresh natural foods prepared as simply as possible. To save both time and money, a baby's meals need to be planned around what the rest of the family is eating, with a minimum of special ingredients or painstaking preparation. It is only in this way that a mother will feel inclined to 'do it herself', instead of falling prey to the tempting convenience and gaily coloured packaging of the ready-made babyfood market.

I do not think anybody would dispute the fact that home-prepared food is superior to tinned and packaged foods, not only nutritionally but also in terms of taste. Fresh food is always best in these respects, no matter how carefully manufactured or additive-free commercial varieties may be. You may well find the latter useful as an occasional standby, and there is certainly nothing easier than opening a jar or adding water to a powder, especially when your baby is only consuming miniscule portions. But stop and consider whether you would feed the rest of the family on an everlasting diet of tinned or dried foods. And, although manufactured babyfoods certainly look attractive, they are expensive, especially when you consider that they are likely to contain a large proportion of sugars, starches and water.

Most babies will consume packaged foods without complaint from the outset (after all, they have never tasted anything else), but if they are used to better fare they may well turn up their noses at such convenience foods. This was demonstrated to me when we took my eldest daughter abroad at the age of nine months. Accustomed to only home-made fare, she protested indignantly when I tried to feed her on the bottled baby foods I had taken along.

Making a proper start

Eating habits are formed remarkably early in life, and research has shown that diet during the first few years has a marked effect on health in later life. It is therefore vital to start your baby off with the best foods, i.e., those which are fresh, wholesome and home-cooked.

The foods to choose for your baby are wholefoods (those that are as natural and unrefined as possible), with an emphasis on lots of fresh fruit and vegetables, and a minimum of fat, sugar and salt.

Do not be deterred if this way of eating sounds foreign to you. Although the ingredients used in this book are wholefood, I am not suggesting that you should radically alter your diet. However, you will find that if you follow the basic principles of healthy eating, as outlined in this book, your whole family will benefit from improved well-being. And for those readers who are new to wholefoods, there is a special section to introduce you to the basic items which comprise a wholefood diet.

Introduce your child to wholefoods right at the start. If he becomes used to eating only this kind of food, much refined food will be unpalatable to him as he grows older. Converting a child from a refined diet to a wholefood one is more difficult, and is best achieved by introducing any changes very gradually.

My aim in writing this book is to show you how easy and enjoyable it can be to prepare your baby's food yourself. It does require a certain amount of forethought, but there is surprisingly little extra effort involved once you get started — the thought is certainly more awesome than the deed. And with the help of this book, I trust that you will be able to overcome any doubts you may have about what and how to feed your baby.

You stand to gain a great deal of satisfaction in feeling that you are doing the best for your baby. Conversely, this makes it all the more vexing if your little one refuses to eat your lovingly prepared food, but I will be showing you ways to minimize potential aggravation.

You do not need a degree in nutrition before you can embark on preparing babyfoods, although a fundamental understanding of the general principles of healthy eating does help. While there is no need to count grams of protein or milligrams of vitamin C, it is essential to serve your baby (and the rest of the family) a balanced selection of foods. You will find more information about planning a balanced diet on page 20.

Similarly, no special gadgets or cooking techniques are called for in the preparation of babyfoods, although the equipment described on pages 12-14 does make life easier.

Preparing your own babyfoods means that you can be much more flexible than with commercial foods. For instance, if your baby is becoming too fat, it is an easy matter to reduce the amount of starchy foods in his diet, simply by cutting down on such items as cereals, bread etc. This is less easy if you are buying prepared foods and are unsure of the exact ingredients. Obesity in babies, by the way, is something to avoid, since there is growing evidence that being fat as a baby predisposes one to fatness later in life (see page 28).

Home-prepared babyfoods are also better socially, since the baby is likely to share family meals from an early age. In fact, I have found with each of my three children that they quickly got to the stage where they would only eat their food if it was the same as the rest of the family was eating!

This book has grown up alongside my third child, Anna, who has acted as a (usually willing) taster for the recipes. But, because babies are individuals, there is of course no guarantee that your baby will enjoy the same foods as mine. However, you will find a sufficient variety of ideas to satisfy even the faddiest of eaters.

You will see that the book is divided into three sections. This is for simplicity's sake, to cover the gradual progression from a baby's first foods, which are simple purées, to the time when he can eat the same as the rest of the family. There are, however, no hard and fast rules about when your baby should progress from one stage to the next, since babies vary enormously in the speed with which they adjust to a solid diet.

However, most babies will be ready to share the family's meals by the time they are 12 months, or at the latest 18 months, old and, since the recipes in the third section can be used indefinitely, it is this which comprises the largest part of the book. Unlike many babyfood books, this third section offers recipes for all the family (all tried and approved by my own family), so that you can continue to use the book long after your baby has grown up.

You will see that I have referred to the baby as 'he' throughout the book. This is not intended as any form of discrimination, but simply avoids the necessity of writing 'he or she' each time.

General Preparation

No particular cooking expertise is called for in preparing babyfoods, and no special techniques are used, with the exception of a few short cuts. However, there is a need to pay special attention to general hygiene, such as always washing your hands before preparing food, and always working with clean cooking utensils.

Before a baby reaches the crawling stage (when anything and everything will probably go into his mouth anyway), it is advisable to sterilize spoons and cups, but other items such as saucepans and bowls need only to be scrupulously clean.

As you read through the book, you will see that the first two stages concentrate on three different methods of food preparation which are designed to minimize the time and effort involved. Using these methods you can have food ready for your baby as and when he needs it, instead of frantically fiddling around with baby-sized portions at the last minute while he is screaming with frustration and hunger — definitely not good for the maternal nerves!

The three methods are as follows:

1. *Fresh:* This encompasses any foods which can be quickly and easily prepared when needed, such as healthy 'convenience' foods like raw fruit, eggs and home-made yogurt.

2. *Quick cooking:* This method relies on two time-saving devices, the first of which is the pregrinding of grains and pulses (see page 36). Both these foods usually require a long cooking time, often preceeded by overnight soaking, but if they are preground the cooking time is shortened dramatically. The resulting powders can be stored in a covered container (a screw-top jar is ideal) in the fridge for up to three months. When you are ready to cook them, simply add three to four parts of water to one of powder, and simmer gently. Pulses and grains will cook in about 10 minutes, with the exception of soya beans, which will need 20 minutes. Add more liquid (which can be water, stock, milk or fruit juice) during the cooking time if necessary, and keep on a low heat to prevent burning. The other short cut method is to finely grate raw vegetables, thereby considerably reducing their cooking time. In this form they can be added to the partially cooked grains and/or pulses, and will cook in a matter of minutes. Try any vegetables that are of the right texture for grating.

3. *Freezing:* If you own a freezer you are fortunate in that an instant source of home-prepared babyfoods is available with a minimum of expenditure and effort. You can cook extra quantities when preparing the family meals and freeze them, or you can cook foods in bulk especially for your baby. In the former case you can prepare all-in-one meals (vegetables and main course all in one portion) while, with the latter, you can take advantage of seasonal offers.

Freezing is second best to fresh as far as nutrients are concerned. Protein, fat and carbohydrate content is unaffected, and there is only a minimal vitamin C loss, with other vitamins and minerals being well retained. Any loss is more than compensated for by the convenience obtained.

For baby-sized portions make use of an ice-cube tray (transferring the cubes to a freezer bag or covered container once frozen) or use small cartons with lids, such as cottage cheese cartons.

When freezing babyfoods it is more than ever important to follow the usual guidelines for freezing, such as using only really fresh foods which are quickly cooked, cooled and frozen. Cover the food while it is cooling or thawing, and never re-freeze food once it has thawed out unless it has been cooked subsequently. The frozen food can be reheated straight from the freezer, or it can be left to thaw in a covered container before heating.

Remember that bacteria thrive under warm conditions, so avoid keeping food warm for any length of time. Similarly, leftovers should be brought to the boil again to kill the bacteria that cause food poisoning.

Equipment

While no special equipment is absolutely necessary for preparing babyfoods, there are some gadgets which do make life considerably easier. Some of these you will probably have already in your kitchen; others you may feel are worth purchasing.

Sieve: Fine mesh, strong enough to withstand considerable pressure as you push the food through. A sieve is useful for foods which are too thick for a blender (e.g., cooked dates), or for foods where pips and/or skins must be removed (e.g., tomatoes). A tea strainer makes a good first sieve for the time when you are coping with minute quantities.

Blender/food processor: These take a lot of the strain out of puréeing foods, but are not recommended for small quantities, since most will adhere to the machine. Also useful for grinding nuts, making breadcrumbs, or soups.

Hand blender: Quicker and more convenient than a conventional blender, this also copes better with smaller quantities without wasting half the food. It is not as powerful, and it is not so easy to obtain a uniform texture with some items, but it has the advantage of being usable in any container, from a saucepan to a mixing bowl. Take extra care to keep this unplugged and away from children, since the blades are easily accessible, and could be lethal if the blender was switched on accidentally.

Garlic press: A bit fiddly to use, but a good way of coping with small quantities of foods with a fairly firm consistency, such as cooked meat. It needs a fair amount of pressure, but a good texture is obtained. If the food you are pressing is very dry, you may need to add a little liquid, but do so with caution since if the food is too sloppy most of it will ooze out the sides of the press.

Grater: An invaluable piece of equipment. Use a fine grater for the early stages, proceeding to a coarser one as your baby progresses to more lumpy foods. A nutmeg grater is good for the very early stages, while a rotary grater works well with cooked meats.

Coffee grinder/wheat mill: Invaluable in the preparation of wholegrains, pulses, nuts and seeds, which can be ground before cooking, thereby drastically reducing the cooking time, and producing foods of a suitable consistency for baby without any need for subsequent puréeing.

Potato masher: Much quicker than a fork, and especially useful when baby is moving on to lumpier foods. Particularly good for soft fruits like pears or peaches.

Steamer basket: This is the most nutritious and tasty way of cooking vegetables, and is a worthwhile investment for all the family. The food sits in a metal basket, designed to fit any saucepan, and is cooked over boiling water in a covered pan. The cooking time is much the same as for boiling, but steaming preserves nutrients which are lost by immersion in water, as well as giving a better flavour, colour and texture. Use the water afterwards for soups or casseroles, or to mix with baby foods.

Introducing Wholefoods

This section is included for the benefit of those readers who are unfamiliar with the wholefood way of eating, and it offers a brief guide to the main ingredients of a wholefood diet.

Eating wholefoods does not mean making any radical changes to your way of life. What it does mean is eating wholesome, unrefined foods, prepared in such a way that they retain as much of their original goodness as possible. You will find that if you follow the advice given below when planning the family's diet, you will see an improvement in the health of all members of the family.

The guidelines to a wholefood diet can best be understood if divided under the two headings: 'eat more' and 'eat less', as follows.

Eat more
Wholemeal flour: This is probably the biggest single change for those new to wholefoods, but it is one that is worth making, not only for improved taste but for better nutritional value. Wholemeal flour, as the name implies, contains 100 per cent of the wheat grain, complete with vitamins A, B, E, protein, unsaturated fat and natural roughage. White flour, on the other hand, loses 'a third of the protein, two thirds of the essential amino acids, and riboflavin, practically all the vitamin A, 80 per cent of the iron and niacin, as well as other members of the B complex' (*British Medical Journal,* 1953). Of these lost nutrients, only four are replaced by synthetic equivalents and there are Government plans

to do away with these as well. Wholemeal flour is also free from additives, unlike white flour, which contains a long list of chemical agents to improve its appearance, texture and keeping properties.

Wholemeal flour is used in just the same way as white, although you may need to add a little more liquid than usual. The different brands vary considerably in texture and behaviour, so it is worth experimenting until you find one that you are happy with. Also available is wheatmeal flour, which contains either 81 or 85 per cent of the wheat grain, compared with 72 per cent in white flour.

Use wholemeal flour for all your baking needs, from cakes and biscuits to sauces and puddings. Look out, too, for products made from wholemeal flour such as wholemeal bread (or, even better, make your own, using a recipe such as the one given on page 154), biscuits and cakes, or pasta. The latter is boiled, as for white pasta, and takes 8 minutes for macaroni, or about 12 minutes for spaghetti.

Wholegrains: Like wholemeal flour, these contain all the goodness of the grain, not just a part of it. Wholegrains are rich in B vitamins, protein, vitamin E and roughage. Into this category come wholegrain breakfast cereals (choose unsweetened varieties), brown rice, and the less well known grains like rye, pot barley, millet and buckwheat.

Fresh Fruit and Vegetables: Eat lots each day to boost your intake of vitamins and minerals. Have some vegetables raw each day in a salad, and try some unusual combinations as suggested on page 123. Minimize the loss of nutrients when cooking vegetables by following the advice given on page 35. It is worth seeking out organically grown produce, since vegetables grown on soil which has been treated with chemical fertilizers and pesticides will be deficient in vitamins and minerals, and may retain potentially harmful chemical residues.

Eat less
Sugar: Unfortunately for those with a sweet tooth, sugar is bad for you, and a high sugar intake has been linked with such diseases as diabetes and coronary heart disease. In Britain we each consume

120 lbs (54.5 kilos) of sugar per year — a figure you may dispute until you add on the sugar 'hidden' in a wide variety of foods, such as baked beans, tomato ketchup, processed meats, tinned vegetables etc. White sugar is the worst of all, since it contributes nothing but calories and, as an unnaturally concentrated food, places an unnecessary strain on the digestion. Raw sugars are only slightly preferable to white, providing as they do small quantities of vitamins and minerals, especially iron, calcium, phosphorus and B vitamins. The most common raw sugars are:

- Demerara: a large, yellow crystal sugar. Buy the raw sugar from the West Indies, not London Demerara, which is simply white sugar dyed brown.
- Muscovado: the least refined of all the sugars, being 88 per cent pure sugar, compared with the 100 per cent of white sugar. Produced in Barbados or Guyana, this is a dark, soft sugar.
- Molasses: similar in appearance to Muscovado, but with a stronger, treacly flavour since it has added molasses.

Cut down on all sugars, and foods containing them. Adding dried fruits to recipes helps reduce the sugar content. In fact you can usually reduce the sugar content in any given recipe by up to half, although do not try it with the recipes in this book, as they have been specially included for their low sugar content.

Honey can be used as an alternative sweetener. It contains the natural sugars fructose and glucose, which are more easily assimilated and less disruptive of blood sugar levels than sucrose (refined sugar). However, it is still sugar, and as such should be used in moderation.

Fats. As in the case of sugar, we eat far too much fat, and the Coronary Prevention Group and Health Education Council recommend people to cut their saturated fat intake by half, and to switch from saturated animal fats to unsaturated vegetable fats. Total fat intake should also be cut by a quarter. A high fat intake, principally of saturated fats, is linked to heart disease and allied complaints, so cut down on greasy or fried foods, and high-fat items like red meat, hard cheeses and cream. Use unsaturated vegetable oils (safflower, sunflower, corn, cottonseed, soya, wheatgerm, sesame and peanut), and polyunsaturated vegetable margarines (e.g. *Flora*), but check the label to make sure they do not contain saturated fats like coconut or palm oil.

Salt. A high salt intake can lead to high blood-pressure and kidney problems. In this country we consume between eight and twelve grams per day, even though we only need a paltry one gram. Use sea salt, which contains a rich balance of mineral salts, and is especially rich in iodine, the mineral essential for correct functioning of the thyroid gland which controls the body metabolism. Sea salt is available in coarse or fine crystals for cooking or grinding in a special salt mill, but get into the habit of adding salt to food only where its taste would be missed, rather than adding it indiscriminately in cooking.

Processed and refined foods. Avoid these as far as possible, since they have had much of their original goodness destroyed, and also contain additives in the form of colourings, flavourings and preservatives. Get into the habit of reading food labels, where ingredients are listed in descending order of weight. Wholefooders limit their use of processed foods to items like canned tomatoes, fish, fruits in natural juice, or tomato purée. With care you can find such items free from preservatives, sugar or salt.

Meat. Limit your consumption of meat to once or twice a week, not only for health reasons, but also because of the cost, and the inhumane way in which most animals are kept. Meat is high in saturated fat, and may contain drug residues. Instead, experiment with alternative sources of protein like fish, nuts, pulses, dairy produce and free-range eggs.

For more guidance on incorporating wholefoods in the diet, see the sample menu on pages 24-25.

The Vegetarian Baby

Bringing your baby up as a vegetarian is easy, and it has the added advantage of eliminating one of the most difficult foods to prepare in a form suited to a young baby. This, combined with the fact that meat is difficult for a baby to digest, might persuade you to delay the introduction of meat until your baby is older, even if you do not intend him to be a vegetarian. There is certainly a case for everyone to eat less meat on the grounds of both economy and health.

There is no need to fear that your baby will go short of essential nutrients or that his health will suffer if you exclude meat from his diet. For, although meat is a good source of protein, it is also likely to contain residues of growth promoters, hormones etc. Meat is also high in fat — of the saturated variety, which is linked to heart disease — and even seemingly lean meat is composed of one-third fat. Tasty meat products like sausages, which so many children seem to enjoy, are much higher in fat than that, as well as containing preservatives, colouring and excessive salt.

If you want to bring your baby up as a vegetarian, the same basic guidelines for a healthy diet still apply (see page 20), but become all the more important. It is not sufficient simply to cut meat out of the diet: you need to improve the quality of the diet overall.

Great emphasis is placed on the need for vegetarians to obtain sufficient protein but, in fact, in the Western world people are more likely to consume too much protein than too little. Some authorities believe that feeding an infant too much protein may actually be harmful, because the body only uses what it needs, with the excess being converted by the liver into glucose. This places a strain on the kidneys, which have to cope with the nitrogen left over as a result of this conversion. Even if consuming too much protein is not actually harmful, it is certainly inefficient, since the process of converting protein to glucose uses more energy than it releases!

The potential deficiencies of a vegetarian diet (protein, calcium, vitamin B_{12} and iron) are avoided if dairy produce is consumed and, with the availability of rennet-free cheeses and free-range eggs, most non-meat eaters are happy to be what is termed 'lacto-vegetarian'.

Before switching to a vegetarian diet, you need to understand the question of complete proteins. Proteins are composed of 21 amino acids, of which eight are termed 'essential' since they cannot be manufactured by man. The body makes most efficient use of proteins which supply all eight of these essential amino acids, i.e., those which are complete proteins. Meat, fish, eggs and dairy produce are all sources of complete protein.

Vegetable proteins, on the other hand, are known as 'incomplete' proteins because they do not contain such a good balance of these eight amino acids, and this means care must be taken to serve more than one type of vegetable protein at a meal to make good any deficiency. Put like that, it sounds extremely complicated, but in fact there are three basic groups of vegetable protein (nuts and seeds; cereals and grains; pulses), and serving any two should provide the body with all the amino acids it needs for building and repairing protein tissue. So it is simply a matter of choosing a menu which contains items from at least two of these categories, and this is, in fact, something which we do instinctively at times. For instance, beans on toast (pulses and grains); bread, biscuits or cakes with added seeds or nuts (grains and nuts/seeds); muesli (grains and nuts/seeds).

Combining a vegetable protein with dairy produce also makes good any shortfall, as when serving cheese on toast, or cereal with milk. While most vegetarians do eat dairy produce, it is best to avoid any over-reliance on these foods which are high in cholesterol (unless you choose low-fat varieties) and mucus-forming (worth avoiding for anyone prone to colds or catarrhal infections).

Iron-rich foods for vegetarians include prunes, molasses, tofu (soya bean curd), split peas, dates, millet, chick peas (garbanzos), spinach, lentils, brown rice, almonds, cashews, dried peaches and apricots. Vitamin C aids the body's absorption of this mineral when both are eaten at the same meal, such as orange juice and eggs for breakfast.

Calcium, for those vegetarians who do not eat dairy produce, is richly supplied in dried fruits (especially figs, apricots and dates), wholegrains, green vegetables, sesame seeds, molasses, carob, and pulses, especially soya.

Vegetarians would be well advised to include in the diet regular servings of the low cost-high nutrition foods and the concentrated sources of nutrients, listed on pages 25-26. Particularly to be recommended are Brewer's yeast, molasses and yeast extract for the B vitamins, and soya flour for additional protein intake.

Many of the recipes included in Stage 3 are suitable for vegetarians, and these are marked with a letter **V**.

A Basic Guide to a Healthy Diet

If you are to provide your baby (and the rest of the family) with a balanced diet, it helps to have at least a basic knowledge of nutrition. This does not mean that you need to memorize long lists of foods rich in a particular nutrient, or to know the precise function of each vitamin, but it does help to know which are the most nutritious foods and why. Do not be deterred by the apparent complexity of the subject for, provided you follow the guidelines at the end of this chapter, you cannot go far wrong.

Foods are comprised of a mixture of nutrients, in widely varying proportions, and each of these nutrients has different functions to perform in the maintenance of health. The nutrients present in food are calories, carbohydrates, fats, protein, vitamins and minerals.

Calories is a word with which most of are only too familiar; this is in fact a measurement of the energy value of food. Calories are present in all foods, and are especially abundant in those with a high carbohydrate or fat content. A certain amount of calories is needed for growth, health and energy but, as many people know to their cost, any excess accumulates in the form of fat.

Carbohydrates are needed by the body to provide heat and energy, being the main source of immediate energy and the only energy source for the central nervous system. If you eat too few carbohydrates valuable protein will be used for energy instead of growth; whereas if you eat too many, the excess will be stored in the body as fat. The answer is to eat a moderate daily amount of carbohydrates, which come in the form of starches and sugars. Natural sources of starch include bananas, wholegrains (and all items made from them such as bread, pasta, cereals, cakes etc.), pulses, potatoes and peas. Natural supplies of sugar are provided by fruit and vegetables especially bananas, peas, apples, carrots, grapes and fruit juices. Although most foods contain more than one nutrient, white sugar is a notable exception, being 100 per cent carbohydrate. This means it is a nutritionally empty food, providing no nutrients while at the same time decreasing the appetite for other more nutritious foods. So, when choosing carbohydrates, it is important to select those with the highest nutritional value.

Fats provide a concentrated source of energy, assist in the absorption of the fat-soluble vitamins A, D, E, and K, and stored fat protects the body from loss of heat, and supports and protects the vital organs. Fats are either saturated or unsaturated, and it is a high intake of the former (chiefly from animal sources) which has been linked with coronary and vascular diseases (see page 16). The main sources of fat in the diet are meats, especially red meats, dairy produce, nuts, and fatty fish.

Protein is the main material for growth and development of many parts of the body, and as such is especially important during the rapid body building of the first years. Opinions vary as to the optimum intake of protein, but in the Western world we are more likely to eat too much than too little. The principal sources of protein in the diet are meat, fish, eggs, dairy produce, nuts, pulses and wholegrains (see page 19 for details of complete and incomplete proteins).

Vitamins are small substances found in all food, and are necessary for both life and health. When vitamins are in short supply all sorts of deficiency symptoms can ensue. All foods contain vitamins in varying amounts, but these substances are mostly very unstable. For instance, storage, processing, heat, water, and air are just a few of the factors which play a part in destroying at least some of the vitamin content of food. This is why many people like to boost their vitamin intake with a regular multivitamin supplement.

- Vitamin A is needed for normal growth, good vision and resistance to infection. A deficiency of this vitamin is particularly common, and is characterized by dandruff and a rough, dry skin. The richest sources of vitamin A are offal, dairy produce, fish liver oils, carrots and fresh green vegetables. Vitamin A is fairly stable under normal cooking conditions.
- The Vitamin B complex consists of more than a dozen individual substances which as a whole are needed for production of energy, and a healthy nervous system, mental state, digestion and skin. The B vitamins as a whole are found in large amounts in wholegrains, pulses, dairy produce, wheat-germ, Brewer's yeast, molasses and offal. Because the B vitamins cannot be stored in the body, a daily intake is essential. All the B vitamins are destroyed by water and heat, so are easily lost during cooking, as well as being destroyed by food processing. The individual vitamins within this group are as follows: B_1 (thiamine); B_2 (riboflavin); B_3 (niacin or nicotinic acid); B_6 (pyridoxine); B_{12} (cyanocobalamine); folic acid; pantothenic acid; biotin; choline; inositol; PABA (para-aminobenzoic acid); B_{15} and B_{17}.
- Vitamin C is needed by all the body cells, being essential for

healthy blood vessels, bones and teeth. It also helps build up resistance to infection, and assists in the healing of wounds or broken bones. Vitamin C cannot be stored in the body and must be supplied daily, since a deficiency can result in frequent infections, a tendency to bruising and bleeding gums. The least stable of all the vitamins, C is destroyed by exposure to air, light, heat, water, storage, use of baking powder, smoking, drugs and stress. The best sources are fresh raw fruit and vegetables, especially blackcurrants, citrus fruits, green peppers, watercress and tomatoes.

- Vitamin D is one of the most important vitamins for babies, since it plays an essential part (along with the minerals calcium and phosphorus) in the formation of teeth, bones and muscles. The main food sources are egg yolk, oily fish, margarine and dried milk powder (the last two are fortified). Vitamin D is also formed by the action of sunlight on the skin.

- Vitamin E's precise function has not yet been established, but it is thought to contribute to normal reproduction and growth, as well as playing a part in maintaining healthy muscles, nerves and skin. Wheatgerm, wholegrains, unprocessed vegetable oils and nuts are the richest dietary sources. The vitamin can be destroyed by heat and exposure to air, and is one of the victims of the refining process used for flours and cereals.

- Vitamin K is a fat soluble vitamin essential for blood clotting and liver function. It is well distributed in foods, especially in green vegetables.

Minerals, like vitamins, are essential to life and health and, although they are only needed in minute quantities, deficiencies are becoming increasingly common. This is because none of the minerals can be manufactured by the body, and they are destroyed by such factors as fertilizers, food processing (especially the refining of flour and cereals), and cooking. These are the principal minerals:

- Calcium is particularly important for growing children, since it plays a major part in the building of strong teeth and bones. The richest source is milk, but other excellent sources are dried fruits, especially apricots, figs and dates; wholegrains; green vegetables; sesame seeds; carob; pulses especially soya; molasses; and oily fish, particularly sardines.

● Phosphorus is linked with calcium, and so is also involved in the formation of bones and teeth. It is found in many foods, especially egg yolk, milk, cheese, nuts and wholegrains.

● Iron is essential for healthy blood, since it combines with protein to form haemoglobin, the substance which carries oxygen around the body. Vitamin C must be plentiful before iron can be properly absorbed. Richest sources are liver, wholegrains, dried apricots, molasses, egg yolk, green leafy vegetables and meat.

● Sodium and potassium work together to maintain the correct fluid balance in the body, making them vital to blood pressure and kidney health. Both are widely distributed in foods, especially in dried fruit, nuts and pulses.

● Iodine is needed before the thyroid gland can function properly, this being the gland which controls the body metabolism. Iodine is present in seafoods, meat and vegetables.

Putting it into practice
If you have plodded through the above, you will have begun to realize that nutrition is an extremely complex subject. So how do you go about providing your family with a balanced diet?

Begin by choosing the best possible basic ingredients — wholefoods, as outlined on pages 14-15. Build on this sound foundation by serving a variety of nutrient-rich foods, such as eggs, dairy produce, fish, nuts, meat (especially offal), and pulses. Include as much raw fresh fruit and vegetables as possible. Add concentrated sources of goodness like wheatgerm, molasses and soya flour.

Putting this advice into practice should produce a family menu roughly along the same lines as the sample menu given below:

Breakfast: fresh fruit juice; muesli or wholegrain cereal (preferably unsweetened), served with fresh or dried fruit, and skimmed milk or yogurt, plus wheatgerm; boiled, poached or scrambled egg; wholemeal bread or toast with honey, no-added-sugar jam, or yeast extract.

Lunch: a mixed vegetable salad incorporating a large variety of leaf and root vegetables, with beansprouts and/or fruit, served with jacket potato, wholemeal bread or crispbread, plus a little cheese, nuts, eggs or meat; yogurt and fresh fruit.

Supper: home-made soup; a protein dish (lean meat, fish, nuts, pulses, grains — including rice dishes, pasta or pastry — eggs or cheese) with lightly cooked (preferably steamed) vegetables; fruit-based dessert (e.g., fruit crumble, fruit fools), fresh fruit or cheese.

Snacks: (see page 52) select from: dried or fresh fruit; hard boiled eggs; apple or carrot pieces dipped in cottage cheese or nut butter; cubes of cheese; wholemeal bread or crispbread with nut butter.

Drinks: mineral water; fresh fruit or vegetable juices; herb teas or weak ordinary tea; decaffeinated coffee or coffee substitute; yeast extract.

You may find it helpful to divide everyday foods into main groups, from which you can include something every day. The more you vary the food from each group, the more balanced the diet will be. These food groups are not to be confused with the food categories for incomplete proteins, as given on page 19.

1. *Protein foods:* meat; poultry; offal; white and fatty fish; eggs.
2. *Dairy produce:* milk; cheese; yogurt.
3. *Cereals and grains:* wholegrains; bread; pasta; pastry; pulses; nuts and seeds.
4. *Fruit and vegetables:* Serve some raw and cooked each day.

Vegetarians will need extra quantities of items from groups two and three.

Low cost, high nutrition foods are soya products; offal; egg yolk; poultry; milk; dry milk powder; leafy green vegetables; carrots; pulses and oranges.

Concentrated sources of nutrients are wheatgerm (see page 43); brewer's yeast (see page 45); molasses (see page 45) and tofu (see page 37).

Recommended daily intake of nutrients for children (U.K. figures)

Age	Protein g	Thiamine Mg	Riboflavin Mg	Mg Nicotinic Acid	C mg	A iu	D iu	Calcium Mg	Iron Mg
0-1 yrs	20	0.3	0.4	5	15	450	10	600	6
1-2 yrs	30	0.5	0.6	7	20	300	10	500	7
2-3 yrs	35	0.6	0.7	8	20	300	10	500	7
3-5 yrs	40	0.6	0.8	9	20	300	10	500	8
5-7 yrs	45	0.7	0.9	10	20	300	2.5	500	8
7-9 yrs	53	0.8	1.0	10	20	400	2.5	500	10

Note: These are the minimum amounts needed to ward off deficiency symptoms — larger quantities are needed for optimum health. Since individual nutrient needs vary widely, tables such as this should only be treated as a guide. Recommended daily intakes also vary from one country to another, e.g., they tend to be much higher than Britain (up to double) in the United States.

Recipe servings
The recipes in Stage Two will make enough for 1-2 servings and for 4 servings in Stage Three, unless otherwise stated.

STAGE ONE

Introducing Solid Foods

The first rule parents must surely learn is that where babies are concerned, there *are* no rules. This applies just as much to feeding as it does to other aspects of babycare since, from the moment they are born, babies are highly complex individuals completely different not only from their peers but also from their siblings.

This discrepancy between babies is reflected in the well-meaning advice offered not only by friends and relations, but also by the many volumes available on babycare. Consult any two people for advice about your baby, and you will almost certainly get two different answers. This can leave the poor parents feeling totally confused and not knowing what to do for the best, but it is really a matter of trial and error to find what is right for your baby. And rest assured that it becomes easier as you and your baby get to know one another better.

The subject of when a baby should first be introduced to solids is a typical one on which opinions vary widely: in my research for this book I have come across extreme examples ranging from three weeks to six months. There are also fashions in baby feeding, as in most things and, whereas my generation was invariably on three meals a day at ten weeks old, such over-indulgence is relatively rare these days.

Current opinion and medical research concur in suggesting that there is no advantage to be gained in starting a baby on solids too young. Indeed, such a move can have an actual detrimental effect on a child's health. Many authorities consider that a baby does not have the necessary enzymes to cope with solids before the age of four months, and there is the added fear that allergies may be provoked because of the immature digestive system, especially where there is a family history of hay fever, asthma or eczema.

A baby who is introduced to solids at an early age is not only deprived of sucking time, but also runs the risk of obesity, a condition to be avoided, since research has shown that a fat baby is likely to become a fat adult, and to have more trouble in losing weight. This is because a fat baby has developed more adipose (fat cells) during his first year, in which case he is likely to get fat and stay fat. Subsequent dieting will reduce the fat content of the cells, but it cannot reduce their number.

A baby can survive in the best of health on a diet formed exclusively of milk until he is six months old, and this is especially true of those babies who are breastfed (two out of every three babies in 1980, compared with one in two in 1979). Once past that age, a baby has increased needs for certain nutrients which cannot be met by milk alone. For instance, he has used up his own store of iron, and so needs to eat foods rich in this mineral.

Taking all the above into account, the best suggestion must be to be guided by your baby. If he is happy and gaining weight, delay introducing solids but aim to do so by six months at the latest. In the majority of cases this will mean starting on some solids by four to five months, but do not begin them before three months, unless yours is an exceptional case. Your baby will probably leave you in no doubt about when he is ready for solids, displaying such tell-tale signs as waking early for his feeds, and sucking hungrily at his fist or fingers.

How to start

When you first start giving your baby solids, it will be some time before he obtains sufficient to satisfy his appetite, as he has first to master the technique of coping with foods in this new form. It is therefore best for your peace of mind to stave off hunger pangs by giving him his milk first, followed by the solids. Give the latter at the feed when he is usually most unsettled, and do not rush him but allow him to suck the food off the spoon. You need to look upon these initial few weeks as a time for experimentation, when you are introducing him to different flavours and textures rather than giving him extra nourishment. After a few weeks, once he comes to terms with the idea, you can change to giving solids first and then topping up with milk afterwards.

When you are introducing your baby to a new food, you should only give him a teaspoonful to start with, in case he should prove to be allergic to it. Do not introduce more than one new food at a time, leaving a gap of several days between each, so that you can identify any offending substance. Once a new food has been accepted, try to include it regularly in his diet so that he becomes accustomed to it. If he seems reluctant to try new foods, try adding a new one to an accepted one to get him used to the taste gradually.

If he has an allergic reaction (such as a rash, sickness or diarrhoea), stop giving him the particular food for a week or two and then try again. It is also a good idea to introduce new foods at the lunchtime feed, in the hope that you will avoid a disturbed night if the food does happen to disagree. Foods that are particularly likely to cause an allergic reaction are egg white (so only the yolk should be given at first), dairy produce, and cereals containing gluten (especially wheat). Other foods which are not suitable for a young baby are rhubarb, pork, oily fish, spicy foods, and fruit with seeds or pips. As you progress with the introduction of solids, it is worth keeping a record of your baby's likes and dislikes and any allergic reactions.

First foods
Many books suggest cereals as a baby's first foods but, unless he is very young or is underweight, there is no good reason for choosing these in preference to anything else. In fact some cereals, especially those containing a lot of gluten as mentioned above, are likely to cause allergies in babies, and most authorities now recommend that babies are kept off these until about eight months

old. This is a point to watch out for if you ever buy packaged baby cereals, since a product you would expect to be free from gluten will often be found to contain wheat if you read the ingredients list carefully. Rye, oats and barley also contain gluten, though wheat is the highest, followed by rye.

Fresh fruits and vegetables are ideal as first foods. Many babies prefer them to cereals anyway, they are less likely to lead to overweight, and they are quickly and easily prepared in the puréed form which a baby requires. They are also cheap to buy if you choose those in season, and some can even be given raw — all they need is to be peeled and mashed.

Babies vary in the speed with which they adjust to solids, but it is worth remembering that the slower the change, the better the baby's digestion will be able to cope. You are, of course, working your way gradually towards three meals a day, and however slow they are at first to get the idea, most babies will be conforming to this pattern by the time they are about nine months old.

Unless your baby is failing to gain sufficient weight there is no need to force food on him, and it is always better to be guided by his appetite than to feel pressured into overfeeding him. Do not be alarmed, therefore, if you read in some babycare book that babies will be doing such and such at a given age — yours may not!

For this reason I have deliberately refrained from including charts to show ages at which to introduce specific foods. Warnings are given where foods should be avoided at first, but otherwise the best advice is to try your baby on a particular food and see whether or not it agrees with him. Some babies happily consume spicy foods, onions and garlic at four months old, while others find even a simple banana indigestible until they are six months old. It all depends on your individual baby and, although it is comforting to be told exactly what to do when, it is also unnecessary, and can be distressing when your baby does not conform to these generalities — as he almost certainly won't do at times.

Once your baby is taking solids successfully at one meal each day, you can begin to add a small amount at a second feed, and follow this some time later by solids at a third feed. Your baby will probably then be having solids plus milk three times a day, as well as a milk feed in the early morning and in the evening. These milk-only feeds are gradually dropped (in whichever order seems appropriate for you and your baby), and the gaps between the remaining three feeds are gradually lengthened so that the pattern roughly becomes breakfast 7-8 a.m., lunch 12-1 p.m., supper 5-6 p.m. This will not necessarily fit in with your baby's wishes, but when he seems ready it is worth trying to alter his habits slightly so that his mealtimes fall into sociable hours and fit in with the rest of the family.

Some babies will happily consume all that they are given, but if you are less fortunate you will have to accept the fact that he does not like all foods, and look for a suitable alternative. A lot of babies eat everything with relish to start with and, just as you are giving yourself a mental pat on the back for producing such a good eater, they suddenly start becoming fussy about their food. This usually happens, without any apparent reason, at about the age of one — a fact I know only too well, since two of my three children suddenly became faddy eaters almost overnight.

Preparing first foods

In this section you will find practical guidance on food categories, with specific instructions for items which need different treatment or which need highlighting (for instance, under 'dried fruits', dates are mentioned separately because they do not need soaking before cooking). Where a food is not mentioned by name, follow the general advice for that particular food category.

No recipes, as such, are required at this stage, since it is simply a matter of providing foods singly or in simple combinations of two or three foods, once your baby is accustomed to each one individually.

The food categories are not listed in any particular order, since it is very much a matter of personal choice as to which foods you prefer to give your baby, and in which order. Your choice will obviously be governed by such factors as seasonal availability, economy and family preferences. To minimize expense and wastage, make use of ingredients you have for the family as much as possible at this early stage. Start off with the individual items from the food categories, and as your baby becomes used to these, offer them in varying combinations. As mentioned earlier, in most cases no specific times are given at which to introduce particular foods, although warnings are issued where certain items should not be given at first.

This section will cover approximately your baby's first two months of solids, but there will inevitably be some overlap with Stage Two, especially for those whose babies take to solids quickly. Once your baby is used to a variety of foods, look at Stage Two as well for further ideas.

Fresh Fruits

Fresh fruits are rich in vitamins A, B, C, with calcium, chromium and some iron, and their natural sugar content makes them easy to digest. However, they need to be ripe and in season for optimum food value. Some fruits, such as bananas, peaches or pears, need no preparation other than peeling and mashing, making them the ultimate in convenience foods. Fruits are best served raw where possible for highest food value, but always remove the skin at first since it is more difficult to digest. If fruit needs cooking to make it more digestible (e.g., cooking apples), bake, stew or steam it. Both raw and cooked fruit purées can be frozen successfully, following the general advice given on page 11.

Apples:
Eating apples are quickly prepared for a baby by peeling and grating very finely (a nutmeg grater is ideal at first). Mix with a little fresh orange juice, and serve at once to prevent discolouration.

Bananas
Only very ripe bananas — those with black spots — should be given since they are otherwise indigestible. Look out for over-ripe bananas at reduced prices at your greengrocers: if you buy a large quantity they can be mashed and frozen.

Citrus Fruits
A bit of a fiddle to prepare, since the peel, pips and most of the pith must be removed, but these are especially high in vitamin C. Use a blender to purée.

Avocado
This is very easy to digest, and is rich in vitamins and minerals, protein and unsaturated fat. It blends well with other flavours such as potato, cottage cheese or fruit, and only needs peeling and mashing. Serve at once to prevent discolouration. Look out for the new mini avocados, which are stoneless and better for baby-sized portions.

Serve raw: Eating apples; bananas; avocados; peaches; pears; melon; dessert plums; grapes (peeled and pipped, then mashed or sieved); very ripe apricots.

Cook first: Cooking apples; plums and apricots (where these are not suitable for eating raw); pineapple (steam for 10-15 minutes unless you have a powerful blender which will cope with it raw).

Avoid until later: Rhubarb; any fruits with seeds or pips. The latter can be given sieved from about seven months, or whole from twelve months; rhubarb from about six months.

As your baby is introduced to the other ingredients, fruits can be mixed with yogurt, egg custard, breadcrumbs or cereals. Fruits combined with vegetables often make the latter acceptable to those who are not keen on vegetables. Try peas and apple, or carrots and apple.

Dried Fruits

These are a good source of minerals, especially iron, calcium, potassium and copper, and of vitamins A, B and C (although they are lower in the latter than fresh fruit). The high fruit sugar content of dried fruit makes it more easily digested than fresh fruit, although it is also higher in calories. Dried fruits, especially prunes, have earned a reputation for being highly laxative, but unless your baby is very young he should be able to cope with a reasonable amount. Other foods, although less well known for their laxative effect, are in fact as high or higher in fibre (for instance, blackberries, raspberries, baked beans, black or red currants, or spinach).

A variety of dried fruits is widely available these days: try your baby on dried apples, pears, apricots, peaches, raisins, sultanas, figs, currants and dates. Most of the above will need to be soaked overnight in water or fruit juice before being cooked and puréed for a young baby. The exception is dates, which only need to be cooked with a little water (about 3 tablespoons to 3 oz/75g dates) for five minutes, or until soft. Press through a sieve to remove skins and fibrous parts.

All the dried fruits have a strong flavour, which makes them good mixers with bland-tasting foods like natural yogurt or wholegrain cereals.

Vegetables

Fresh vegetables are another excellent source of essential vitamins and minerals, and the darker the colour of the vegetable, the more nutritious it is. Top of the list as far as nutritive value is concerned are broccoli, spinach, sprouts, peas, asparagus, artichokes, cauliflower and carrots.

As with fruit, serve as many vegetables as possible raw, either puréed or very finely grated. Finely grating vegetables before cooking them substantially reduces the cooking time, or you may prefer to cook them first and then purée them.

The way in which vegetables are cooked is very important, since poorly cooked vegetables will lose a large proportion of their vitamin and mineral content. Minimize nutrient loss from vegetables by buying produce as fresh as possible, preferably organically produced or home grown, and the darker in colour the better. Leave vegetables unpeeled wherever possible (e.g., peel potatoes to be mashed after boiling) since much of the goodness is in or just under the skin. Store vegetables in a cool, dark place; do not soak in water; and chop up immediately prior to cooking. Cook in the minimum amount of liquid (vegetables do not need to be immersed) and use this afterwards for drinks, soups or casseroles since it will contain water soluble nutrients. Always put vegetables into boiling water, and cook for the shortest possible time — vegetables should retain some crunchiness and not degenerate into a soggy mass.

Steaming (see page 13) is one of the best methods of cooking vegetables, or you can wrap them in foil and bake in the oven at 325°F/170°C (Gas Mark 3). Steaming will take about the same time as boiling, while baking will take from 20 minutes for sprouts or cauliflower, to 35 minutes for whole carrots or 45 minutes for whole parsnips. Freeze vegetables raw or cooked and puréed.

Beansprouts are extremely nutritious, being rich in vitamins C, A, E, K, B_2, B_6, folic acid, calcium, iron and magnesium. They are easy and cheap to grow at home (see page 122). Purée the raw sprouts with other ingredients, adding a little liquid if necessary, or cook lightly first.

Serve raw: Puréed or finely grated carrots, celery, cucumber (peeled), beetroot (this can cause red stools or urine so do not be alarmed!), tomatoes (peel, and sieve to remove seeds), beansprouts.

Serve cooked: Any of those mentioned above, plus peas, potatoes, spinach, green beans, broad (Windsor) beans, courgettes (zucchini), parsnips, swede (rutabaga).

Avoid at first: Sweetcorn, mushrooms. Strong-tasting vegetables like those of the brassica family (cabbage, broccoli, cauliflower etc.) and onions may cause wind: if so, delay for a further month.

The dark green leafy vegetables may be full of goodness, but they are often unpopular. If so, try one of the following methods: purée with milk after cooking; leave the saucepan lid off for the first few minutes of cooking to give a milder flavour; blend raw or cooked green vegetables with egg and milk and then scramble.

Pulses

These dried vegetables are a good source of protein, iron and B vitamins. Do not be deterred from serving them by the thought of pre-soaking and long cooking, since you can take one of two short cuts. Either cook extra when preparing them for the family, then purée and/or sieve to remove the skins at first. Or grind the raw pulses in a grinder or wheat mill, which cuts the cooking time right down to 10 minutes, or 20 minutes for soya beans. To cook in this way, add three to four parts of liquid to one part of pulses.

Some books suggest introducing pulses from four months old, while others recommend leaving them until nine months old. Once again, the best advice is to be guided by your baby, so that if you know he has a delicate digestion you would tend to leave it later than if he appears to cope well with whatever you give him.

A wide variety of pulses is available these days in supermarkets or health food shops, and if you are not familiar with cooking them, any vegetarian or wholefood cookbook will help. Stage Three also gives recipes incorporating pulses. Most common among the pulses are butter (Lima) beans, lentils (whole or split), haricot (navy) beans, kidney beans, chick peas (garbanzos) and soya beans.

Tofu, or soya bean curd, is a concentrated source of protein, and supplies many other nutrients, including calcium and iron. It is also free from cholesterol, low in calories (52.6 per 100 grams), and easy to digest. It has a bland flavour, which not only means most babies will enjoy it, but also makes it a good mixer with either savoury or sweet foods. Adults can use it to make salad dressings, dips or spreads, or add it to soups, casseroles or puddings.

Soya flour is another very concentrated source of protein. It mixes well with all sorts of foods, for instance mix with an equal quantity of water and stir into fruit or vegetable purées. In baking you can add two tablespoons of soya flour to each ½ pound (500g) of flour, or you can use it to replace eggs, in which case one tablespoon of flour is equivalent to one egg.

Eggs

As already mentioned, only the yolk is given at first, since the white can sometimes cause an allergic reaction. The white in fact has little nutritive value other than protein, but whole eggs are a good source of iron, vitamins A, B complex (especially B_{12} and biotin), D, E, copper, calcium and phosphorus. Free-range eggs are slightly higher in some nutrients, besides tasting better and involving no cruelty in the way the hens are kept.

Egg yolks can be added to hot foods (for instance, vegetables) and will cook through in the heat; or they can be hardboiled and then sieved and diluted with a little milk, stock etc. An unsweetened custard is quick and easy to make, and mixes well with other foods, whether savoury or sweet. Simply beat together

¼ pint (125ml/⅔ cup) milk and one egg yolk, and heat very gently until fairly thick. Do not overheat or it will curdle — if this does happen, blend in a liquidizer. Cool and store in a covered container in the fridge, where it will keep for a few days.

If you want to use yolks only instead of whole eggs in other recipes, bear in mind that one yolk is equal to one whole egg, for instance in a custard recipe or for most baked goods. Scrambled egg using the yolk only is made in the usual way, by adding a little milk or water, and cooking over a low heat in a little melted butter or vegetable margarine. Scrambled egg makes a good vehicle for leftovers, such as fruit, vegetables, meat, grated or cottage cheese, cereals or rice.

Milk

Once a baby is about five months old he can drink cow's milk from the bottle, but it should be diluted fifty-fifty with boiled water until he is about eight months old. Milk and other dairy produce are a common cause of allergy, so watch closely for any reaction. For further advice on milk, and on alternatives, see the drinks chapter on page 166.

Yogurt

Yogurt can be introduced earlier than milk, since it is more easily digested, and is less likely to provoke an allergic reaction. This appears to be because the lactose content of the milk (the substance to which children allergic to cow's milk are usually intolerant) is converted to lactic acid. However, some children will also be allergic to yogurt, so watch for a reaction when first introducing it.

Yogurt is high in protein, B vitamins, and calcium. Home-made yogurt is extremely easy to make at a fraction the cost of bought yogurt, and it has a delicious bland flavour (see page 100 for instructions). There are endless ways of using yogurt: for instance, mixed into vegetable or fruit purées, with cereals, or used in place of milk for cooking, such as for sauces or scrambled egg. If cooking with yogurt take care not to overheat it or it will curdle.

You can also make a tasty, low-fat, soft yogurt cheese by straining yogurt through a piece of muslin (a clean muslin nappy is ideal). Leave it hanging overnight, or for a shorter time, depending on what consistency you require. This cheese is nice for adults too if flavoured with herbs and/or garlic, and is ideal for cooking, such as in cheesecakes.

Cheese

Cottage cheese, like yogurt, is often tolerated earlier than milk but check the labels for the one with the least amount of additives (health food shops may well be the best source). Sieve cottage cheese at first to give a smoother texture, and thin with a little liquid if necessary. It is a good mixer with fruits, vegetables, cereals etc.

Cheese is a good source of protein, calcium (about seven times as much as milk), phosphorus, vitamin A and riboflavin. Most hard cheeses have a high fat content and so should be used in moderation, but exceptions are Edam, Gouda, Gruyère and Mozzarella. Introduce your baby to cheese by finely grating it and stirring it into vegetables, cereals or savoury dishes. Young babies often find cheese easier to digest if it is served in this way rather than being cooked.

Meat

As explained in the chapter on vegetarianism (page 18), meat is a good source of high quality protein, B vitamins and trace minerals, but it may also contain traces of growth hormones and chemicals. This, plus the high price it commands and the difficulty involved in preparing it in puréed form, may convince you to delay introducing it until your baby can eat foods of a coarser consistency.

For ease of digestion, meat should be introduced in the following order: white meats (e.g., chicken); organ meats (e.g., liver); red meats (e.g., lamb or beef); pork. Prepare meat in puréed form by scraping raw lean meat with a sharp knife, and cooking the resulting paste in a cup standing in a pan of boiling water. Cook until the meat changes colour, and add a little liquid before or during cooking if a moister consistency is required.

The easiest way to prepare meat for a baby is to use a portion of the family meat which has been grilled or roasted (not fried), and to purée it with vegetables to make a meal in one that can then be frozen.

Liver is a highly nutritious food, and an excellent source of iron, so it is worth including it in the diet regularly if your baby will eat it. Some children dislike the taste, but might eat chicken liver which is milder in flavour, or liver disguised in home-made pâtés. Rather than frying liver for a baby, steam it for ten to fifteen minutes, or grill it for three or four minutes on each side.

Fish

Fish makes a good early food for babies, since it is easy to digest and is low in fat. It is also a good source of vitamins and minerals, especially iodine, phosphorus and magnesium.

Avoid oily fish such as mackerel and sardines at first, but it is worth introducing them by the time he is seven or eight months old since they are very nutritious. Steam fish for a baby for ten to 15 minutes; bake it in the oven at 350°F/190°C (Gas Mark 4); or grill it for five to ten minutes on each side, adding a little milk if necessary. Check and recheck the cooked fish for bones, then flake it with a fork or purée it in a blender.

Cereals

As stated earlier, cereals are best introduced after fruits and vegetables have been established for several weeks, and those containing a lot of gluten should be delayed until as late as eight or nine months where there is any family history of allergies. Current thinking certainly suggests leaving wheat, which has the highest gluten content, until that age. For ease of digestion, start with rice or millet, followed by barley, oats, rye and wheat, in that order.

Each of these cereals offers different nutrients (see below), so it is worth incorporating a variety in the diet.

- Rice: B vitamins, calcium, phosphorus, iron.
- Millet: very high in iron (three times as much as other cereals), good protein, B_1, B_{17}, minerals.
- Barley: good protein and silicic acid, the most important mineral in building up the nervous system and sense organs.
- Oats: the highest in protein and fat, with magnesium, iron and several B vitamins, especially B_1.
- Rye: similar to barley in protein, fat and carbohydrate content, but also contains vitamin E, potassium, magnesium, and unsaturated fatty acids.

- Wheat: high in protein, vitamins E, B, A and calcium.
- Buckwheat: rich in vitamin C and calcium.

These are, of course, the nutrients present in the whole grain, and processed cereals (such as most breakfast cereals, white rice, pearl barley) no longer contain the most nutritious parts of the original grain. Your baby can cope with wholegrains by the time he is five or six months old, although it may give him looser stools than previously (if they are too loose, leave the cereals for a few weeks and then try again).

The easiest and quickest way to prepare wholegrains for a baby is to grind them in a coffee grinder, wheat mill or powerful blender. It sounds fiddly, but a few minutes grinding can give you enough cereal for three months. Store them in an airtight container in the fridge for up to three months. Cook the grains by mixing approximately three parts of liquid to one of grain, and simmer gently for five to ten minutes. The cooked cereal will keep for a few days in the fridge, or can be frozen. It can be used straight from the freezer by steaming for a few minutes, or by adding to other purées before heating through — almost as easy as opening a packet, and a lot better for your baby. Vary the taste by cooking the cereals with different liquids, such as fruit juice, vegetable stock, yogurt, milk or water. The cooked cereals can also be used to thicken up sloppy foods.

This pre-grinding cuts down considerably on the cooking time, but if you have no means of grinding there is no need to be deterred from preparing wholegrains for your baby. You can soak the grains overnight and then cook them, in which case it is best to prepare a large quantity, or use some left over from the family's meals, and then purée and freeze the cooked cereal.

Cooking times and quantities of liquid are as follows:

Rice: 2 cups of liquid to 1 cup of rice. Cook for 30/40 minutes.

Millet:
Barley: } 2 cups of liquid to 1 cup of cereal.
Rye: } Cook for 20/30 minutes.
Oats:

Wheat: 3 cups of liquid to 1 cup of wheat. Soak overnight and cook for about 1 hour.

Buckwheat: 1½ cups of liquid to 1 cup of buckwheat. Cook for 30 minutes.

To make porridge for your baby, simply cook ground oatmeal or rolled oats with milk as detailed above, and then purée if necessary. There is a good baby muesli on the market, or you can make your own with the recipe on page 56.

Bread: Once your baby is used to eating cereals bread can form a regular part of his diet, but this should be wholemeal bread which is made from 100 per cent wholemeal flour, complete with vitamins A, B, E, protein, unsaturated fat and natural roughage. Home-made bread is undoubtedly the best of all, since you know just what is in it, and since even wholemeal bread is allowed to contain a certain number of emulsifiers, stabilizers and preservatives. A recipe for easy breadmaking is given on page 154.

Making your own bread also means you can include a few hidden nutritious extras, such as soya flour, eggs, or wheatgerm (see below). Breadcrumbs are useful for thickening sloppy foods (wholemeal breadcrumbs soaked in milk make an instant cereal if time is short), or use squares of toast for soaking up soups.

Wheatgerm is part of the grain which is removed during the refining process for white flour, even though it is the most nutritious part, being rich in protein (28 per cent), and nearly all the vitamins, especially A, B and E, unsaturated fat and minerals.

Wheatgerm is invaluable for thickening baby foods (grind it at first if an even finer texture is required), and it can be used in recipes in place of breadcrumbs, as well as in baking, and casseroles. Raw wheatgerm is preferable to the toasted variety, since the cooking process will have destroyed some of the nutrients. Keep raw, or unstabilized, wheatgerm (as it is also known) in the fridge once it has been opened to prevent it going rancid.

Nuts and Seeds

These foods are high in unsaturated fat, and are a good source of protein, vitamins B and E, calcium, iron, potassium, magnesium, phosphorus and copper. They are indigestible for babies in their raw state, but can be introduced at an early age in the form of nut or seed milks (see page 170). The baby can then progress to ground nuts (use a grinder, a rolling pin or a pestle and mortar). Later, once he can chew, he can have larger pieces and is then ready to eat nut butters.

The seeds referred to are sunflower and sesame, either of which can be eaten raw, or lightly toasted before adding to salads or casseroles, or used in baking.

Tahini is a sesame seed paste which is rich in vitamin E, protein, phosphorus, and potassium, and is especially high in calcium. It can be mixed with sweet or savoury dishes from an early age.

Carob

Chocolate is not a suitable food for babies (or for anybody else for that matter!), being high in sugar and saturated fat. Carob is a natural alternative which has a similar taste to chocolate, but is high in calcium, and is free from the stimulants caffeine and theobromine which are present in chocolate. Carob (which is produced from the bean of the carob, or locust, tree) is naturally sweet, and supplies vitamins A, D and B (especially B_1, riboflavin and niacin), and minerals potassium, magnesium, phosphorus, copper and iron. In powdered form carob is used like cocoa, or it can be purchased in bars like chocolate.

Concentrated Sources of Nourishment

These are foods which give improved quality for less quantity, such as wheat germ (see Cereals); soya flour (see Pulses); and seeds (see Nuts and Seeds). Also under this heading come the following:

Brewer's Yeast: Rich in protein, minerals and B vitamins, often with B_{12} added. Its strong taste may make it unacceptable to babies, but you can try adding a little of the powder to drinks or incorporate it in baking. My children were introduced to yeast tablets from an early age, and happily chew their way through them each morning, which is something I could never do!

Molasses: This is the brown syrup which is left in the refining process when sugar crystallizes, and it is rich in vitamins and minerals, especially iron. It has a similar taste to treacle although somewhat stronger, and it can be used sparingly in baking or drinks.

Milk powder: This is a good source of protein, and you can boost the protein content when baking by adding two tablespoons to each cup of liquid used.

Points to Remember

Sweetening: Remember that a sweet tooth is usually cultivated rather than inherited, and try to discourage your baby from developing one by keeping sweetening to a minimum. A baby will often happily consume a food that seems sour to you. Remember that all sugar, whatever the colour, is bad for you, and that honey is also a sugar and so should be used in moderation (see page 15).

Ready-prepared babyfoods still contain a large proportion of sweetening, even though manufacturers have reduced the amount, because they claim sugar must be added to food to make it palatable to adults. One brand of rusks, which declares itself to be low in sugar, still contains 18 per cent sucrose. It is a pity British manufacturers cannot follow the example set in America where, in 1977, Heinz removed sugar from all its babyfood varieties except those where it was really needed.

Seasoning: Avoid adding salt and pepper to your baby's foods. The food may taste bland to you, but will seem normal to your baby who is not used to eating seasoned foods. Salt puts a strain on the kidneys, and a high intake has been linked with high blood pressure and heart disease (see page 17).

Consistency: It is important to obtain food of the right consistency, as your baby may have trouble coping with foods that are too runny or too thick. Thin foods by adding fruit juice, milk, yogurt or vegetable cooking water. Thicken foods by adding sieved or mashed hard-boiled egg yolk, soya flour, cooked cereals, milk powder, wheatgerm or breadcrumbs.

Travelling: If you are going out somewhere and need to take your baby's foods with you, the following is an easy way of coping with any contingency. Make up his food as thick as possible. Take a flask of boiling water with you, and use this to get the food to the right consistency and temperature when mealtime comes. Or get your baby used to eating cold foods!

Vitamin supplements: Your health visitor may advise you to give your baby vitamin drops from an early age and, while this does offer insurance against any deficiency, it is worth remembering that a carefully planned diet of wholesome foods is always preferable to synthetic vitamins. You can also boost your baby's vitamin intake by giving him such vitamin-rich foods as wheatgerm, brewer's yeast and yeast extract.

Drinks: For advice on how and when to give your baby drinks, please see page 166.

Finger foods: Once your baby starts teething and/or begins to put everything into his mouth, he is ready to start on finger foods. More details about these are given on page 50.

STAGE TWO

Moving on to Meals

This second stage begins when your baby is used to a wide variety of foods, and is ready to move on to slightly more elaborate meals. His foods will still be presented in puréed form, and indeed even at this stage the simplest way to plan his meals is to work on the basis of blending different combinations of purées. Once again, you can make use of frozen purées, and short-cut cooking methods such as the pre-grinding and grating recommended in the first stage.

As with the introduction of solids, there is no set age at which your baby should progress to this stage, since it depends on his digestion, and the age at which he first started solids. It will be very roughly two months after his first tastes of solids, but there is inevitably some overlap between the first two stages, so it is worth consulting Stage One as well. Again, you should take your cues from your baby, and avoid any temptation to rush him on to eating quantities and types of food for which he is clearly not yet ready.

As you extend the range of foods your baby can eat, so his meals come closer to following the basic composition of those eaten by the rest of the family. This is certainly something to encourage, because if you can serve him the family food in puréed form it makes the planning and preparation of babyfoods easier, and it includes your baby in the family circle at mealtimes from an early age. As your baby grows older he will quickly learn to prefer what the rest of the family is eating anyway — it always looks so much tastier than his own food!

In a sense this second stage is the most fiddly one as far as catering is concerned, since it requires more imagination and forethought than were needed during the early stage when only tastes of food were being given. However, if you follow the basic principle of giving your baby the foods to which he is already accustomed, and continuing to add new ones (with caution as before), you can come up with any number of new food combinations. Some will naturally be more successful than others, but it is worth remembering that babies will often eat food combinations which adults would find unpalatable. This is because they have no preconceived ideas about what should or should not be eaten together. For instance, a baby will often enjoy sweet and savoury foods combined, such as carrots and apples.

There is in fact no need to produce an enormous variety of menus for your baby, bearing in mind that you should aim for a mixed wholefood diet, as outlined in the sections on wholefoods and nutrition. If you follow the guidelines given above, and add a little imagination, you can easily think up all sorts of new ideas. Examples are included in this section, but they are intended as a starting point only, to encourage you to be adventurous in preparing your baby's foods. Remember that natural foods taste good on their own, and even though they may sometimes seem lacking in flavour to you, your baby is not used to sugar, salt and spices.

As suggested in Stage One, it is well worth keeping a list of which foods your baby likes and dislikes, and which combinations worked well or not. Then, if you are stuck for ideas one day, it is a simple matter to refer to the list.

Thinking up what to feed your baby becomes easier anyway as he grows older and is able to eat more foods. By the time he is about a year old you should find that he is able to cope with most foods, although there may be one or two that he still finds difficult to digest, such as pork, spicy foods, or fruit with seeds or pips (unless sieved).

As at all other stages of feeding a baby, you need to be guided by his natural appetite. The amount he eats is likely to vary widely from one day to another, but provided he is neither under- nor overweight, is growing well and is normally active, there is no cause for concern. A baby's growth rate in fact slows down during the second half year, and there is evidence to suggest that overfeeding during the first year alters the actual chemistry of the body, including the number of fat cells (see page 28), and resulting in an increase in the production of insulin (which metabolizes sugars) and growth hormones.

Finger foods

Once your baby starts cutting his first teeth and starts putting everything in his mouth, it is time to provide him with hard foods to chew on. These finger foods aid the formation of healthy teeth and gums, and soothe him during teething. Finger foods not only encourage independence and interest in food, but they are a good step towards feeding himself, and they offer an opportunity for him to try different tastes and textures.

A baby who is still eating food in puréed form from a spoon will often accept lumpy foods (such as diced vegetables) if he is able to pick them up and eat them himself. Hard items which might cause choking should be avoided, and for this same reason a baby should never be left unattended with finger foods.

Any of the following make suitable finger foods:

- *Rusks*, home-made (see recipe, page 80).
- *Wholemeal biscuits* (digestives are a good texture, being one of the few kinds which do not just crumble, or disintegrate into a soggy mess).
- *Eggs:* scrambled; hard-boiled and chopped; or omelettes, chopped.
- *Fruit:* pieces of raw peeled fruit such as pear, banana, peach. Apple can cause choking, so give in pieces large enough to chew on but not to swallow.
- *Cheese:* grated, or cottage cheese.
- *Fish:* small pieces of cooked fish, but check extra carefully for any bones.

- *Meat:* finely chopped or minced chicken or other meats.
- *Cooked pasta:* chopped if necessary.
- *Vegetables:* raw or cooked (e.g., carrots or peas). If giving raw carrot, give in large pieces he can gnaw on but not swallow, or he may choke.
- *Cooked pulses.*
- *Pieces of dried fruit:* unsoaked, such as apple ring, apricot, or pear.
- *Miniature sandwiches:* with a soft filling, such as cottage cheese, yeast extract, no-added-sugar jam.
- *Wholegrain cereals:* ready to eat, served dry (look for varieties without added sugar).

Moving on from purées

Once your baby has a few teeth (or even before they appear if he is late in cutting them), you can begin to serve his food mashed or finely chopped rather than in smooth purées. If your baby seems reluctant to accept food in this way, the transition can often be eased by combining equal quantities of puréed and mashed or chopped food. You can then gradually decrease the proportion of puréed food as you step up the other. Do not try to rush this change over, or he may rebel!

As your baby becomes accustomed to foods in lumpier form, gradually try introducing him to the salads which form a major part of a wholefood diet. Try him on peeled and deseeded tomatoes, peeled cucumber, grated carrot, chopped celery, raw beansprouts, and other vegetables which can be served raw in salads.

It is usually at about this time that the question of eating between meals first crops up, especially when plates of biscuits seem to be provided wherever you go. Obviously it would be difficult, if not impossible, to deny him them when they are there in front of him, but at home it is best to discourage eating between meals, especially of biscuits or sweets (this applies equally to other members of the family).

Not only does this habit diminish the appetite by filling one up with nutritionally poor foods, but it also contributes to tooth decay. Research has shown that it is the number of times that sugar enters the mouth that is the prime cause of decay. In fact, the less sugar that is consumed in the early years the better, for if a child loses his back milk teeth prematurely through decay his first permanent molars may break through the gum too far forwards, and leave too little room for the permanent front teeth, which will then come through crowded and out of line.

If your baby needs sustenance between mealtimes, choose snacks with a good balance of nutrients, such as fresh fruit or raw vegetables, wholemeal bread with cottage cheese or peanut butter. Give such snacks half way between meals, offering water or fruit juice to drink rather than milk, since the latter stays in the stomach for much longer, and so is likely to decrease his appetite for his next meal.

The following recipe section contains both specific recipes for your baby, and some ideas for food combinations. The latter are intended to spark off your imagination, and although specific quantities are given these are by no means obligatory, since the amounts can be varied according to the proportions and consistency required.

It is difficult to be precise about quantities for babies at this stage, since appetites can vary widely, but the recipes should make one to two servings unless otherwise stated. Where a recipe makes more than one serving, the unused portion can be kept in a covered container in the fridge for two to three days, or can be frozen. It can then be reheated over a gentle heat, stirring and adding a little liquid if necessary; or can be placed in a covered container and steamed over boiling water until heated through. Recipes which are not suitable for keeping, such as those containing avocado or banana, are given in quantities for one serving only, as indicated in individual recipes. Remember to keep separate any food you wish to store: do not keep any leftovers from the bowl from which you have been feeding your baby.

Many of the recipes in Stage Three are also suitable for this age, and these are marked with the (2) symbol, together with any specific instructions for adapting them to a baby's needs.

Breakfasts

The following recipes are equally suitable for desserts, especially when cereal has not been given at breakfast time. Other more traditional breakfasts that are also suitable for a baby include wholegrain cereals (preferably unsweetened); fresh fruit and yogurt; porridge; eggs, poached, scrambled or boiled; wholemeal bread or toast, cut into squares and spread with yeast extract, honey or no-added sugar jam.

Banana Oats

Imperial (Metric)	American
2 oz (50g) ground oats	½ cup ground oats
¼ pint (125ml) milk	⅔ cup milk
½ banana, sliced	½ banana, sliced
2 fl oz (60ml) natural yogurt	¼ cup natural yogurt

1. Cook the oats in the milk for 5 minutes, stirring occasionally.

2. Meanwhile blend together the banana and yogurt and stir in. Cook for a few more minutes to heat through. Serve at once.

Rice and Fruit

Imperial (Metric)
1 oz (25g) ground brown
   rice
¼ pint (125ml) milk or fruit
   juice
3 tablespoons fruit purée
Honey to taste (optional)

American
¼ cup ground brown rice
⅔ cup milk or fruit juice
3 tablespoons fruit purée
Honey to taste (optional)

1. Cook the rice in the liquid for 5-10 minutes adding more liquid
   if necessary and stirring occasionally.

2. Stir in the fruit purée and the honey, if required. Serve hot
   or cold.

Date and Orange Delight

Imperial (Metric)
2 tablespoons ground cereal
   (e.g., barley or rice)
Juice of 1 orange
1 oz (25g) dates, finely
   chopped
2 teaspoons honey

American
2 tablespoons ground cereal
   (e.g., barley or rice)
Juice of 1 orange
¼ cup dates, finely chopped
2 teaspoons honey

1. Cook the cereal with the juice and dates for 5-10 minutes,
   adding more liquid if necessary and stirring occasionally.

2. Stir in the honey. Serve hot or cold.

Fruity Cereals

Using pre-ground cereals (see page 42) and finely chopped dried fruit, soaked overnight, you can prepare many different variations in a matter of minutes. You will need at least five tablespoons of liquid to one of grain, and the liquid can be varied; for instance, fruit juice, milk, yogurt or water. Keep an eye on the cereal during cooking, as you may need to add more liquid. Try the following combinations to start you off. Each is cooked for 5-10 minutes, stirring occasionally, and can then be puréed if wished (a hand blender is ideal) and served hot or cold.

- Imperial (Metric)
  2 tablespoons ground oats
  1 tablespoon ground
    almonds
  1 oz (25g) finely chopped
    dates
  ¼ pint (125ml) apple juice

  American
  2 tablespoons ground oats
  1 tablespoon ground
    almonds
  ¼ cup finely chopped
    dates
  ⅔ cup apple juice

- 2 tablespoons ground rice
  4 dried apricots, soaked
    overnight in the
    cooking liquid and then
    chopped fine*
  ¼ pint (125ml) natural
    yogurt

  2 tablespoons ground rice
  4 dried apricots, soaked
    overnight in the cooking
    liquid and then chopped
    fine*
  ⅔ cup plain yogurt

*If the dried apricots are at all sharp, add a little honey to taste.

- 2 tablespoons ground
    barley
  1 oz (25g) raisins, soaked
    overnight in the
    cooking liquid
  ¼ pint (125ml) nut milk
    (see page 170)

  2 tablespoons ground
    barley
  2 tablespoons raisins,
    soaked overnight in the
    cooking liquid
  ⅔ cup nut milk (see page
    170)

Baby Muesli (1 serving)

Imperial (Metric)

2 teaspoons each of ground oats, millet, wheatgerm and toasted nuts

1½ tablespoons milk or fruit juice

½ small eating apple, finely grated

American

2 teaspoons each of ground oats, millet, wheatgerm and toasted nuts

1½ tablespoons milk or fruit juice

½ small eating apple, finely grated

1. Mix together the grains and nuts and soak overnight in the liquid.

2. Stir in the freshly grated apple, and serve at once.

Eggs and Cheese

Cheese and Rice Whip (2-3 servings)

Imperial (Metric)	American
2 tablespoons pre-ground brown rice	2 tablespoons pre-ground brown rice
¼ pint (125ml) milk	⅔ cup milk
1 egg, separated	1 egg, separated
2 oz (50g) grated cheese	½ cup grated cheese
1 tablespoon wheatgerm	1 tablespoon wheatgerm

1. Cook the rice with the milk for 5 minutes, stirring occasionally.

2. Remove from the heat and stir in the egg yolk, cheese and wheatgerm.

3. Beat the egg white until stiff but not dry, and fold into the rice.

4. Put in a greased shallow ovenproof dish and bake at 350°F/180°C (Gas Mark 4) for 35 minutes, or until puffy and golden. Serve at once. This is one that is tasty enough to serve to other members of the family too.

Cheesey Potatoes (2-3 servings)

Imperial (Metric)
1 medium potato
1 oz (25g) grated cheese
1 egg yolk
2 tablespoons milk

American
1 medium potato
¼ cup grated cheese
1 egg yolk
2 tablespoons milk

1. Cook the potato until tender, peel and mash.

2. While still hot stir in the other ingredients and cook for a few minutes over a very low heat.

Cheese and Tofu Sauce

Imperial (Metric)
1 tablespoon tofu
1 tablespoon finely grated cheese
1 tablespoon boiling water
2 tablespoons puréed or mashed cooked vegetables

American
1 tablespoon tofu
1 tablespoon finely grated cheese
1 tablespoon boiling water
2 tablespoons puréed or mashed cooked vegetables

1. Mix together tofu, cheese and water, stirring well until cheese melts.

2. Stir in the vegetables, heat through and serve.

Cottage Eggs

Imperial (Metric)
2 oz (50g) cottage cheese
1 egg, beaten
1 tablespoon fresh
    wholemeal breadcrumbs

American
¼ cup cottage cheese
1 egg, beaten
1 tablespoon fresh
    wholewheat breadcrumbs

1. Stir all the ingredients together.

2. Put into a small greased ovenproof dish and bake at
    350°F/180°C (Gas Mark 4), for about 20 minutes, or until set.
    Serve hot or cold.

Cheesey Rice

Imperial (Metric)
4 tablespoons cooked brown
    rice
2 tablespoons cottage cheese
2 tablespoons milk
1 tablespoon beansprouts

American
4 tablespoons cooked brown
    rice
2 tablespoons cottage cheese
2 tablespoons milk
1 tablespoon beansprouts

1. Blend all the ingredients together, adding more milk if
    necessary.

2. Sieve if a smoother consistency is required.

Cheese and Egg Custard (1 serving)

Imperial (Metric)	American
1 egg, beaten	1 egg, beaten
¼ pint (125ml) milk	⅔ cup milk
2 tablespoons grated cheese	2 tablespoons grated cheese

1. Mix all the ingredients together and put in a greased ovenproof dish.

2. Bake at 350°F/180°C (Gas Mark 4), for about 30 minutes, or until set.

Cottage Cheese Plus

Cottage cheese is an excellent mixer with both sweet and savoury foods. For instance, try the following combinations, each of which provides one serving:

- 1 tablespoon cottage cheese
  1 tablespoon apple purée
  1 tablespoon finely chopped beansprouts
- 1 tablespoon cottage cheese
  1 tablespoon cooked dates
  2 tablespoons cooked mashed carrots
- 1 tablespoon cottage cheese
  1 tablespoon stewed apple
  2 teaspoons wheatgerm
- 2 teaspoons cottage cheese
  1 teaspoon smooth peanut butter
  ½ banana, mashed
  2 teaspoons stewed apple

Pulses

Lentil Savoury

Imperial (Metric)
2 tablespoons ground lentils
6 tablespoons water or
    vegetable stock
1 small carrot, finely grated
2 tablespoons grated cheese
1 tablespoon wheatgerm
    (optional)

American
2 tablespoons ground lentils
6 tablespoons water or
    vegetable stock
1 small carrot, finely grated
2 tablespoons grated cheese
1 tablespoon wheatgerm
    (optional)

1. Cook the lentils with the water or stock for 5 minutes, stirring occasionally. Add the carrot and cook for a further 5 minutes.

2. Add the cheese and cook over a gentle heat, stirring, until cheese melts. If mixture is too sloppy, add wheatgerm to thicken.

Bean Bake

Imperial (Metric)
4 tablespoons cooked pulses, mashed
1 small carrot, cooked and mashed
1 tablespoon wheatgerm
1 egg yolk
¼ teaspoon yeast extract

American
4 tablespoons cooked pulses, mashed
1 small carrot, cooked and mashed
1 tablespoon wheatgerm
1 egg yolk
¼ teaspoon yeast extract

1.   Mix all the ingredients together and put in a greased shallow dish.

2.   Bake at 350°F/180°C (Gas Mark 4) for 20 minutes or until set.

Bean and Courgette (Zucchini) Roast

Imperial (Metric)
2 oz (50g) courgettes, steamed and mashed or puréed
2 tablespoons baked beans
1 egg yolk
2 teaspoons fresh wholemeal breadcrumbs

American
2 ounces zucchinis, steamed and mashed or puréed
2 tablespoons baked beans
1 egg yolk
2 teaspoons fresh wholewheat breadcrumbs

1.   Mix all the ingredients together and put in a greased shallow dish.

2.   Bake at 350°F/180°C (Gas Mark 4) for 20 minutes.

Cheesey Beans

Imperial (Metric)	American
2 tablespoons baked beans	2 tablespoons baked beans

1 tablespoon fresh
    wholemeal breadcrumbs
	1 tablespoon fresh
	    wholewheat breadcrumbs

1 tablespoon grated cheese	1 tablespoon grated cheese
1 egg yolk	1 egg yolk

1. Mash the beans and stir in the other ingredients.

2. Cook gently over a low heat for a few minutes, stirring, until mixture thickens.

Beans and Cereal

Imperial (Metric)	American
2 tablespoons baked beans	2 tablespoons baked beans
1 tablespoon ground millet	1 tablespoon ground millet
5 tablespoons milk	5 tablespoons milk

1. Mash the beans. Cook the millet with the milk for 5 minutes, stirring occasionally.

2. Stir in the beans and heat through.

To vary:
Use different kinds of pulses and/or cereals, and substitute stock or tomato juice for the milk.

Grains and Nuts

All the following suggestions for grains rely on pre-ground cereals (see page 42), which are cooked in combination with pulses and/or fresh vegetables. In each case one part of the cereal is cooked with 5 parts of liquid (stock, milk or tomato juice) for 5 minutes, stirring occasionally. The other ingredients are then added for a further 5 minutes, with extra liquid being added if necessary. The following combinations each provide 1 serving:

- 1 tablespoon brown rice
  1 tablespoon cooked mashed pulses
  ½ stalk of celery, finely chopped
  1 teaspoon tahini
- 1 tablespoon brown rice
  1 tablespoon ground lentils (add with the rice)
  ½ small eating apple, peeled and grated
- 1 tablespoon millet
  2 teaspoons ground lentils (add with the millet)
  ½ courgette (zucchini), finely chopped
- 1 tablespoon barley cooked with milk
  2 teaspoons grated cheese
  1 tablespoon peas
- 1 tablespoon millet
  1 tablespoon finely chopped beansprouts
  3 green beans, finely chopped
- 1 tablespoon barley
  ½ celery stalk, finely chopped
  3 green beans
  ½ teaspoon chopped parsley
- 1 tablespoon barley
  1 small carrot, grated finely
  1 tablespoon cottage cheese

Endless variations on the above can be obtained by using different cereals and vegetables in different combinations. If you do not want to grind cereals, you could substitute cooked wholegrain cereals.

Simple Nut Roast

Imperial (Metric)
2 tablespoons finely ground
  nuts
2 tablespoons fresh
  wholemeal breadcrumbs
1 tablespoon wheatgerm
½ teaspoon unsalted tomato
  purée
½ teaspoon chopped parsley
1 egg, beaten

American
2 tablespoons finely ground
  nuts
2 tablespoons fresh
  wholewheat breadcrumbs
1 tablespoon wheatgerm
½ teaspoon unsalted tomato
  paste
½ teaspoon chopped parsley
1 egg, beaten

1. Mix together all the ingredients and put into a greased ovenproof dish.

2. Bake at 350°F/180°C (Gas Mark 4) for 15-20 minutes. Serve hot or cold.

Vegetables

Simple Soup (makes about ⅓ pint/200ml/¾ cup)

Imperial (Metric)
2 oz (50g) mixed vegetables
¼ pint (125ml) milk, tomato
juice or vegetable stock

American
2 ounces mixed vegetables
⅔ cup milk, tomato juice or
vegetable stock

1. Steam the vegetables until tender and purée with the liquid until smooth.

2. Serve with squares of wholemeal bread or toast to soak up the soup. This is a good way in which to disguise vegetables for those babies who are not keen on them.

Vegetable Custard

Imperial (Metric)
3 oz (75g) mixed vegetables
4 tablespoons milk
1 egg, beaten

American
3 ounces mixed vegetables
4 tablespoons milk
1 egg, beaten

1.   Steam the vegetables until tender, and mash. Meanwhile beat
     together the milk and the egg. Stir in the vegetables, pour
     into a greased shallow dish, and bake at 350°F/180°C (Gas
     Mark 4) for 35 minutes or until set.

Carrot and Tahini Bake (2-3 servings)

Imperial (Metric)
1 small potato
1 small carrot
1 egg, beaten
1 teaspoon tahini (see page
   44)

American
1 small potato
1 small carrot
1 egg, beaten
1 teaspoon tahini (see page
   44)

1.   Steam the vegetables until tender, and mash. Stir in the egg
     and tahini.

2.   Put in a small ovenproof dish and bake at 350°F/180°C (Gas
     Mark 4) for 25 minutes.

Tomato Casserole

Imperial (Metric)	American
4 tablespoons fresh wholemeal breadcrumbs	4 tablespoons fresh wholewheat breadcrumbs
4 tablespoons grated cheese	4 tablespoons grated cheese
3 tomatoes, peeled, deseeded and chopped	3 tomatoes, peeled, deseeded and chopped
1 teaspoon chopped parsley	1 teaspoon chopped parsley
2 tablespoons cottage cheese	2 tablespoons cottage cheese

1. Mix together the crumbs and grated cheese and mix the tomatoes and parsley. Put layers of tomatoes and breadcrumb mixture in a small ovenproof dish, finishing with the crumbs.

2. Cover and bake at 350°F/180°C (Gas Mark 4) for 20 minutes. Stir in the cottage cheese and bake for a further 10 minutes. This makes a delicious accompaniment for adult meals too.

Avocado Mix (1 serving)

Imperial (Metric)	American
2 small potatoes	2 small potatoes
3 green beans	3 green beans
1 oz (25g) avocado	1 ounce avocado
2 tablespoons unsweetened egg custard (see page 37)	2 tablespoons unsweetened egg custard (see page 37)

1. Steam the potatoes and beans until tender.

2. Peel and mash the potatoes, and finely chop the beans.

3. Stir in the mashed avocado and the custard, and heat through gently. Serve at once.

Vegetable Variety

You can obtain any number of different flavours by combining different vegetables with one another and adding extras like tofu, cheese, egg, yogurt or tahini. For instance:

- 1 small carrot, cooked and mashed
  1 tablespoon raisins, soaked overnight and then drained
  2 tablespoons natural yogurt
- 2 ounces (50g) broccoli, cooked and mashed
  1 tablespoon cooked peas
  1 tablespoon tofu
  ½ teaspoon chopped parsley. If necessary thin with 1 tablespoon unsweetened custard (see page 37)

Both the above provide one serving only.

Meat

Macaroni Mince (2-3 servings)

Imperial (Metric)	American
2 oz (50g) minced beef	¼ cup ground beef
4 tablespoons water or stock	4 tablespoons water or stock
1 oz (25g) wholemeal macaroni, cooked and drained	¼ cup wholewheat macaroni, cooked and drained
1 oz (25g) Edam cheese, grated	¼ cup grated Edam cheese
3 tablespoons milk	3 tablespoons milk

1. Brush a pan with oil, and brown the meat quickly over a high heat.

2. Add the water, cover and simmer for 20 minutes.

3. Add the macaroni and the cheese and stir until cheese melts.

4. Add the milk, and mash or purée as required.

Apple Chicken or Liver

Imperial (Metric)
*1 chicken breast, skinned, or
4 oz (100g) lambs' liver,
sliced*
*1 eating apple, peeled, cored
and sliced*
¼ pint (125ml) apple juice

American
*1 chicken breast, skinned, or
4 ounces lambs' liver,
sliced*
*1 eating apple, peeled, cored
and sliced*
⅔ cup apple juice

1. Put all the ingredients into a pan and bring slowly to the boil.

2. Cover and simmer gently until meat is cooked — about 15 to 20 minutes for the liver, or 25-30 minutes for the chicken.

3. Chop or purée as required.

Meat and Veg

If you remove a portion of the family's meat after cooking, you can combine it with a variety of different vegetables to come up with endless new combinations. The easiest way to do this is to keep a selection of cooked vegetables in the freezer (see page 11). Try the following to start you off:

- 2 tablespoons finely chopped chicken
  2 tablespoons cooked brown rice
  1 small carrot, steamed and mashed
- 2 tablespoons finely chopped chicken
  1 small potato, steamed and mashed
  2 tablespoons finely chopped beansprouts
  2 tablespoons unsweetened egg custard (see page 37).

Such combinations as those given above can be mashed or puréed, according to the stage your baby has reached.

Fish

Kedgeree

Imperial (Metric)
1 tablespoon pre-ground
  brown rice
5 tablespoons milk
2 tablespoons flaked tuna or
  cooked white fish
1 egg, hard-boiled

American
1 tablespoon pre-ground
  brown rice
5 tablespoons milk
2 tablespoons flaked tuna or
  cooked white fish
1 egg, hard-boiled

1.   Cook the rice with the milk for 5 minutes, stirring occasionally,
     and adding more milk if necessary.

2.   Stir in the fish and the finely chopped egg.

To vary:
Substitute 2 tablespoons cooked brown rice, mixing with the fish
and egg, and adding only enough milk to bind together.

Salmon Bake

Imperial (Metric)	American
1 tablespoon pre-ground brown rice	1 tablespoon pre-ground brown rice
5 tablespoons water or stock	5 tablespoons water or stock
1 small carrot, finely grated	1 small carrot, finely grated
2 tablespoons tinned salmon, flaked	2 tablespoons canned salmon, flaked
1 egg, beaten	1 egg, beaten

1. Cook the rice with the liquid for 5 minutes, stirring occasionally and adding more liquid if necessary.

2. Add the carrot and cook for a further 5 minutes.

3. Stir in the salmon and the beaten egg, and cook over a gentle heat for 2-3 minutes until mixture thickens.

Fruity Fish

Imperial (Metric)
2 oz (50g) white fish fillet
Juice of ½ orange
Squeeze of lemon juice

American
2 ounces white fish fillet
Juice of ½ orange
Squeeze of lemon juice

1. Preheat the grill to high. Put the fish in a shallow greased dish, pour over the juices, and grill for 5 minutes on each side.

2. Flake the fish and check carefully for bones before serving.

Desserts

The best and undoubtedly the easiest dessert to prepare is fresh fruit, puréed or mashed and served with natural yogurt, egg custard (see page 37), soya flour, or tofu (one part of tofu to two of fruit). For those occasions when you want to give your baby a treat, here are some wholesome dessert recipes, all of which are based on fresh fruit.

Fruit Mousse

Imperial (Metric)
6 tablespoons fruit purée
1 egg yolk
2 tablespoons natural yogurt
Honey to taste (optional)

American
6 tablespoons fruit purée
1 egg yolk
2 tablespoons natural yogurt
Honey to taste (optional)

1. Mix together the fruit purée and the egg yolk and heat slowly, stirring, until the mixture boils.

2. Remove from the heat at once and stir in the yogurt. Add a little honey if required, and chill for a few hours until thick. Try serving this to all the family: just increase the quantities.

To vary:
Fold in the stiffly whisked egg white.

Cheese and Fruit Blend

Imperial (Metric)	American
1 banana, sliced	1 banana, sliced
2 oz (50g) cottage cheese	¼ cup cottage cheese
2 tablespoons orange juice	2 tablespoons orange juice

1. Mix all the ingredients together and purée until smooth. Serve at once. Good enough for all the family.

To vary:
Use other fruit in season.

Apple Nut Bake

Imperial (Metric)	American
4 oz (100g) cooking apples	4 ounces cooking apples
2 teaspoons orange juice	2 teaspoons orange juice
1 egg yolk	1 egg yolk
1 tablespoon ground almonds	1 tablespoon ground almonds

1. Peel, core and slice the apple, and cook with the orange juice until soft.

2. Mash or purée, stir in the egg yolk and almonds, and bake at 350°F/180°C (Gas Mark 4) for 15 minutes or until set. Serve hot or cold.

To vary:
Use other fruit in season.

Fruit Custard

Imperial (Metric)
1 piece of fruit, chopped
1 egg yolk
3 tablespoons milk

American
1 piece of fruit, chopped
1 egg yolk
3 tablespoons milk

1. Put all the ingredients in a liquidizer and blend until smooth.

2. Pour into a small greased ovenproof dish, stand in a tin of water, and bake at 350°F/180°C (Gas Mark 4) for about 45 minutes, or until set. Serve hot or cold.

Fruity Bread Pudding

Imperial (Metric)	American
¼ pint (125ml) milk	⅔ cup milk
1 heaped tablespoon fresh wholemeal breadcrumbs	1 heaped tablespoon fresh wholewheat breadcrumbs
2 teaspoons soya flour	2 teaspoons soy flour
2 tablespoons fruit juice	2 tablespoons fruit juice
1 egg yolk	1 egg yolk

1. Bring the milk to the boil, remove from the heat, and stir in the breadcrumbs. Leave to stand for a few minutes.

2. Meanwhile, mix together the soya flour and fruit juice until smooth. Stir into the breadcrumbs with the egg yolk and pour into a lightly greased ovenproof dish.

3. Cover with foil and bake at 350°F/180°C (Gas Mark 4) for about 40 minutes, or until set. Serve hot or cold.

Note: The pudding may look slightly curdled when hot but it tastes fine, and the texture improves as it cools down.

Breads, Biscuits and Cakes

You are unlikely to want to bake especially for your baby, since most ordinary recipes will be suitable, but rusks and teething biscuits are two items that are well worth making.

Savoury Rusks
I find that these are popular with all the family, not just the baby!

Imperial (Metric)	American
4 slices wholemeal bread	4 slices wholewheat bread
1 teaspoon yeast extract	1 teaspoon yeast extract
4 tablespoons boiling water	4 tablespoons boiling water

1. Cut the bread into fingers or squares. Dissolve the yeast extract in the water, and brush onto all sides of the bread.

2. Put on a baking tray and bake at 300°F/150°C (Gas Mark 2) for about 1 hour, until really crisp and dry.

3. When cool, store in an airtight container.

To vary:
Sweet Rusks may be made in exactly the same way, by substituting 1 teaspoon of honey for the yeast extract: this gives just a slight hint of sweetness.

Teething Biscuits (makes about 16)

A fairly soft, chewy biscuit which is good for gnawing on!

Imperial (Metric)
5 tablespoons wholemeal
  flour
5 tablespoons soya flour
1½ tablespoons runny
  honey
½ egg yolk
1 tablespoon vegetable oil
Milk to mix

American
5 tablespoons wholewheat
  flour
5 tablespoons soy flour
1½ tablespoons runny
  honey
½ egg yolk
1 tablespoon vegetable oil
Milk to mix

1. Mix all the ingredients together, adding just enough milk to make a stiff dough.

2. On a floured surface roll out to ¼ inch (5mm) thick and cut into fingers.

3. Place on a greased baking sheet and bake for 15 minutes at 350°F/180°C (Gas Mark 4). When cool store in an airtight container.

STAGE THREE

Family Fare

When your baby is ready to progress to this final stage catering suddenly becomes considerably easier, for this is the point at which he begins to eat the same as the rest of the family. There will still be occasions when your meals are not suitable for him, but most recipes can be readily adapted for a baby, for instance, by removing his portion before adding spices.

This is the largest recipe section of the book because it is the one which will cover the greatest part of your baby's childhood years. The early stages of preparing special babyfoods pass amazingly quickly (even though they seem interminable at the time) and, by the time he is one year, or, at the latest, eighteen months old, a baby can really be considered as one of the family when it comes to mealtimes.

In this section you will find recipes that are suitable for all the family, so you can continue to use them long past the time your baby is tiny. Most of the recipes are those which have proved popular with all members of my family, so I hope that the result is more imaginative than standard nursery fare. And although one or two may sound familiar, all are made with wholefood ingredients.

During the toddler years a child's appetite can vary enormously for no apparent reason and, as already mentioned in Stage Two, it is often at around the age of one that a child suddenly becomes choosy about his food. At this sort of age there is often a natural decrease in appetite since the rapid growth rate of the first year slows down during the second and third years. If your child is not eating normally you should also consider other possible causes for his loss of appetite, such as teething, illness, too many snacks between meals, or the fact that he is getting more satisfaction out of refusing food than eating it.

Having said that, it is important, as at other stages, to be guided by your child's appetite rather than trying to force food on a child who is obviously not hungry. Keep servings small and offer second helpings rather than overwhelm the child with an overladen plateful. Since this is also the age at which a child is becoming increasingly independent, trying to force a child to eat can all too easily result in feeding problems. And if you consistently give a child more food than he wants, you will soon get into a pattern where he refuses more and more, and before you know it mealtimes will have become a battlefield.

The best indications that a child is getting enough of the right foods are his general appearance, contentment and weight gain. It is surprising how some children thrive on remarkably little food and, provided your child is healthy and you only offer him a variety of *healthy* foods, there is no need to worry about the amount he eats.

However, for many mothers their child's eating is a constant source of worry, and in extreme cases the whole family's life can be disrupted by it. The toddler, who is looking for ways to assert himself and his individuality, quickly discovers that mealtimes are a good place to attract attention and get mother running round in ever-decreasing circles.

The easiest way to cope with feeding problems is to avoid them in the first place. As already mentioned, children very quickly learn that not eating is a good way of getting extra attention, so a relaxed attitude on your part is vital. This is a lot easier said than done, as anybody who has been in this situation will know, but dividends will be quickly paid by firmness and calmness.

The first and most important thing you must do is to convince yourself that your child will not starve to death! Any worry on your part, however well concealed you imagine it is, will be picked up by your child, and he should never be made to feel that he is eating to please you, or that you are worried if he refuses food.

You can be helped considerably in adopting this mental attitude if you have the reassurance of knowing that you are serving only wholesome foods. In this way, even if he does eat only a small amount, at least you can be sure that what he does eat is doing him good.

An interesting experiment on feeding children only natural foods was conducted by Dr Clara Davis in the 1930s, and it is still equally relevant today. She set out to discover what children would eat if they were given free choice of wholesome foods. The study involved 15 children, aged between six and eleven months, who had previously only been breastfed. The children were offered a selection of wholesome foods, such as vegetables, fruit, eggs, cereals, meat, wholegrain bread, milk, water and fruit juice.

During the following year all the children developed very well, with none of them becoming either too fat or too thin. And although their appetites varied widely from one meal to the next, and they sometimes went on binges of a particular food or ate unorthodox combinations, over a period of time each chose a well-balanced diet. Indeed, in two cases where the babies had shown signs of rickets at the outset, both actually chose foods high in calcium.

As a result of this experiment, which lasted up to four years with some of the children, Dr Davis concluded that an unspoiled child's appetite can be trusted, provided he is offered a reasonable variety and balance of natural unrefined foods that he enjoys eating.

So, having satisfied yourself that you are providing such a well-balanced diet, try to remain outwardly calm and appear to ignore whether or not your child is eating his food. Accept the fact that there will be some foods he dislikes and look for suitable alternatives, but do encourage him to try new tastes too. Fussing over a food may turn a temporary dislike into a permanent hate — a fact I can substantiate only too well from my own childhood, since I still detest the Brussels sprouts I was forced to eat!

At all costs resist the temptation to beg or threaten at mealtimes, or to express annoyance, hard though this may be. Make it clear to your child that he will be having nothing more to eat until the next mealtime, and keep this up without weakening your resolve. Use similar tactics if mealtimes are becoming more and more protracted as he plays around with his food. If he does eat up properly, express your approval by offering extra attention and affection rather than a concrete reward.

One of the most common food problems must be when the child refuses to finish his first course, but eagerly demands his dessert. There are several ways in which to tackle this problem, but it is worth being aware of the fact that if you say 'no pudding until you have finished', you increase his desire for the pudding, which is the exact opposite of what you want to achieve.

If he consistently wants the pudding but not the main course, you could try reversing the order in which you serve them, especially if the dessert is fresh fruit. I have found one of the most successful methods to be one of compromise. Once the child starts saying he has had enough of his first course, and providing he has made a genuine effort to eat some, I make two piles, one he must eat and one he can leave. It is up to you to decide the proportions of the two piles.

If you do encounter feeding problems, you need to take the pressure off your child, and aim to make mealtimes as pleasant as possible. Encourage the child's eagerness for food by serving only what you know he likes for a while, and by offering smaller quantities. At this stage it is certainly not worth preparing elaborate meals which he is unlikely to eat, since this will only make you more frustrated.

You should, however, aim for a mixed diet so that he is more or less sharing what the rest of the family is eating. Idiosyncratic diets (e.g., all cereal, or all bread and cheese) are to be strongly discouraged, since this means the child has become far too aware of what he eats as a focus of your attention. However, be prepared to make some concessions to his dislikes, for instance by offering an alternative vegetable, or by disguising eggs in puddings, pancakes, cakes or custards.

Doing it himself

At about the time he is ready to share in the family meals your child may well show an interest in feeding himself, and provided you can turn a blind eye to the mess, this is certainly to be encouraged. Not only does it help him to become more independent but, if he is allowed this degree of self-determination, he will eat the amount he needs and nutrition is less likely to become confused with discipline.

Continuing to feed your baby with a spoon not only tends to make him lazy but also decreases his interest in food. Better to buy a bib with sleeves, cover the floor with a plastic mat if necessary, and let him get on with it. He may allow you to help him with a second spoon to start with although, if he is the independent type, he is more likely to push you away.

At this stage it helps to prepare food of a sufficiently thick consistency so that it does not all run off the spoon before he has a chance to get it to his mouth. A useful way to thicken foods that are too sloppy is to bind them with sauce (e.g., white, cheese or parsley); or you could add wholemeal semolina, breadcrumbs, or cooked wholegrain cereals (see page 41).

It is probably during the pre-school years, as your child becomes more independent and outgoing, that you begin to realize what you are competing with as far as food is concerned. You may be lucky and live in a community where other mothers show equal concern for their child's diet, but the odds are that you will feel rather out of the ordinary, surrounded by mums who dole out refined foods, sweets and sugary squash with never a second thought.

Some well-meaning folk may even go so far as to suggest that your 'cranky' diet is actually doing your child harm and, while you stand little chance of convincing such diehards of your point of view, you can at least rest assured that you are doing the best for your child. Confronted with such criticism, it is usually best to offer a simple statement in defence: that you feed your family on wholefoods, which are as near to their natural state as possible, and are free from artificial additives, which may have a detrimental effect on health.

This situation becomes most marked when your child starts visiting friends' houses for meals, or starts eating school dinners. There is little you can do to control what he eats when he is away from home but, hopefully, a few years of healthy eating, together with a simple explanation of why you eat the way you do, will influence his tastes. I have certainly found this to be the case with the more refined and sugary foods, which my children refuse to eat if offered when away from home. That is not to say that they will not eat and enjoy some of the foods that they are not offered at home, but at least their basic diet is a wholesome one.

For nutritional information on the different ingredients used in the following recipes, please consult Stage One, and the sections Introducing Wholefoods and A Basic Guide to a Healthy Diet.

Breakfasts

It may come as news to those who do not eat breakfast, but this is really the most important meal of the day, and it can make all the difference to how you feel during the day. This is because during the night the level of sugar in the blood falls dramatically. If you do not 'break your fast', the level will continue to fall during the morning, leaving you feeling tired and lacking in energy and concentration.

But if you eat the right combination of foods at breakfast time, your blood sugar level will return to normal, and will remain there throughout the morning. This fact has been demonstrated by a number of surveys on the subject, including several on school children, who were found to work better and concentrate more if they had eaten a good breakfast.

The ideal mixture of foods is small quantities of carbohydrate and fat with a moderate amount of protein. Too much carbohydrate and sugar (such as that provided by refined cereals) has the effect of raising the blood sugar dramatically, but only temporarily.

For guidance on planning a balanced breakfast, see the suggested menu on pages 24-25, and try out some of the recipes that follow.

Muesli V

There are many variations on this traditional Swiss breakfast dish, so it is really a matter of trial and error to find one that your family likes. Here is one that is popular with mine:

Imperial (Metric)	American
1 lb (500g) mixed flaked grains (e.g., barley, rye, millet, oats) or muesli base	2 cups mixed flaked grains (e.g., barley, rye, millet, oats) or muesli base
8 oz (250g) mixed dried fruit, chopped	1⅓ cups mixed dried fruit, chopped
2 oz (50g) raisins	⅓ cup raisins
3 oz (75g) chopped nuts	⅔ cup chopped nuts
3 tablespoons sesame seeds	3 tablespoons sesame seeds
3 tablespoons sunflower seeds	3 tablespoons sunflower seeds
1 oz (25g) dried milk powder	1 tablespoon dried milk powder
1 oz (25g) wheatgerm	¼ cup wheatgerm

1. Mix all the ingredients together and store in an airtight container.

2. Serve with lots of fresh fruit, and milk or yogurt. Some people prefer muesli if it has been soaked overnight.

Granola (makes 1½ pounds/750g) V

Granola is another popular wholegrain cereal, this time of American origin. It is based on oats, but in this case they are roasted with the other ingredients to give a crunchy texture. Homemade granola works out much cheaper than the bought variety, and is delicious served with milk or yogurt, as a topping for desserts, or even eaten by the handful as a snack.

Imperial (Metric)	American
10 oz (300g) porridge oats	2 cups porridge oats
4 oz (100g) chopped nuts	1 cup chopped nuts
3 tablespoons vegetable oil	3 tablespoons vegetable oil
9 tablespoons clear honey	9 tablespoons clear honey
4 oz (100g) raisins	⅔ cup raisins
4 oz (100g) wheatgerm	1 cup wheatgerm
1 teaspoon natural vanilla essence	1 teaspoon natural vanilla essence

1. Mix all the ingredients together. Spread ½ inch (1cm) thick on a greased baking sheet, and cook at 275°F/140°C (Gas Mark 1) for about 50 minutes, or until golden brown. Stir occasionally to prevent burning.

2. Leave to cool, break up into chunks, and store in an airtight container.

Mixed Grain Porridge (serves 4) V2

Imperial (Metric)
3 oz (75g) porridge oats
1 oz (25g) flaked wholegrains
(e.g., wheat, rye, or barley)
2 tablespoons ground
almonds or other nuts
2 tablespoons raisins
1 pint (500ml) milk and
water mixed

American
¾ cup porridge oats
⅔ cup flaked wholegrains
(e.g., wheat, rye, or barley)
2 tablespoons ground
almonds or other nuts
2 tablespoons raisins
2½ cups milk and water
mixed

1. The night beforehand, place all the ingredients in a saucepan, stir well, and leave to soak overnight.

2. The next morning, bring gradually to the boil, stirring, and simmer gently for about 10 minutes until thick and creamy. Serve with a little extra milk poured over.

Fruity Oatmeal Porridge (serves 4) V2

Imperial (Metric)
3 oz (75g) oatmeal
2 oz (50g) dried apricots,
  chopped
2 oz (50g) raisins
1 pint (500ml) mixed water
  and milk

American
¾ cup oatmeal
½ cup dried apricots,
  chopped
½ cup raisins
2½ cups mixed water and
  milk

1. Follow the instructions given opposite for Mixed Grain Porridge.

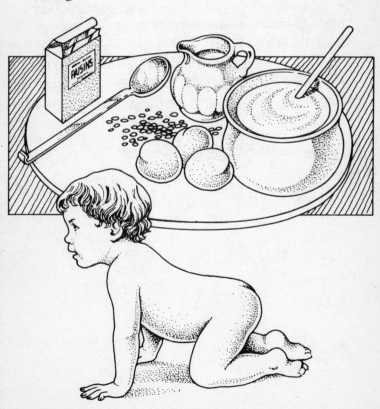

Orange Muffins (makes 12) V2

Only for those who get up early, but definitely worth the effort once in a while.

Imperial (Metric)	American
1 large egg, beaten	1 large egg, beaten
¼ pint (125ml) orange juice and milk, mixed	⅔ cup orange juice and milk, mixed
2 teaspoons melted butter	2 teaspoons melted butter
2 oz (50g) wholemeal flour	½ cup wholewheat flour
Grated rind of ½ orange	Grated rind of ½ orange

1. The night before, make the batter by beating together the egg, liquid and butter. Add the flour and orange rind and beat well.

2. Cover and store in the fridge overnight.

3. Preheat the oven to 450°F/230°C (Gas Mark 8). Stir the batter, and put into lightly oiled bun trays. Bake for 10 minutes, then reduce the temperature to 400°F/200°C (Gas Mark 6), and bake for a further 10 minutes, until crisp and well risen.

4. Serve hot with no-added-sugar jam, or honey.

Cheese, Eggs and Yogurt

Although both eggs and cheese appear frequently in recipes in all the sections, the following are where they form the principal ingredients.

Cheesey Toast (serves 4 as a snack) V2

Imperial (Metric)
2-3 thick slices wholemeal
  toast
1 egg, beaten
¼ pint (125ml) milk
4 oz (100g) grated cheese
4 spring onions, chopped
  (optional)

American
2-3 thick slices wholemeal
  toast
1 egg, beaten
⅔ cup milk
1 cup grated cheese
4 scallions, chopped
  (optional)

1. Cut toast into ½ inch (1cm) cubes and put in a greased shallow pie dish.

2. Beat the rest of the ingredients together and pour into the dish.

3. Bake in a preheated oven at 400°F/200°C (Gas Mark 6) for 20 to 30 minutes, until risen and golden. Serve at once.

For a baby:
Omit the spring onions (scallions) if preferred.

Wholemeal Pizza (serves 4-6) V2

This can also be made using an ordinary bread dough, but I have found the following to give a much lighter, softer crust. It freezes successfully, either when ready to bake or after cooking. If freezing uncooked, place the frozen pizza in a hot oven and bake for about 35 minutes.

Base:

Imperial (Metric)	American
½ oz (15g) fresh yeast	1¼ tablespoons fresh yeast
5 tablespoons warm water	5 tablespoons warm water
2 oz (50g) butter or margarine	¼ cup butter or margarine
8 oz (250g) wholemeal flour	2 cups wholewheat flour
½ teaspoon sea salt	½ teaspoon sea salt
1 egg, beaten	1 egg, beaten

Topping:

Imperial (Metric)	American
14 oz (400g) tin tomatoes, drained	14 ounce can tomatoes, drained
1 onion, sliced	1 onion, sliced
6 oz (150g) Edam cheese, grated	1½ cups grated Edam cheese
1 teaspoon dried oregano	1 teaspoon dried oregano
1 tablespoon oil	1 tablespoon oil
Optional extras: olives; sliced mushrooms; chopped green pepper	Optional extras: olives; sliced mushrooms; chopped green pepper

1. Mix the yeast with the warm water.

2. Rub the fat into the flour and salt until mixture is crumbly. Add the yeast liquid and the egg and mix to form a stiff dough.

3. Knead for a few minutes on a lightly floured surface, then place in a floured bowl, cover with oiled polythene, and leave until double in size (about an hour in a warm place, or 1½ hours at room temperature).

4. Knock back the dough and roll out to fit a greased 12 inch (30cm) round tin or a rectangular tin, about 9×12 inches (23×30cm).

5. To make the topping, liquidize the well-drained tomatoes with the sliced onion. Spread over the prepared dough. Top with the cheese and sprinkle on the herbs and oil. Add any extras used. Leave to prove for 15 minutes.

6. Bake at the top of a preheated oven 425°F/220°C (Gas Mark 7) for 20 minutes.

For a baby:
Keep a small portion of the pizza free from herbs.

Cheesey Sausages (serves 4) V2

For the sausages:

Imperial (Metric)	American
5 oz (125g) wholemeal breadcrumbs	2½ cups wholewheat breadcrumbs
4 oz (100g) mature Cheddar cheese, grated	1 cup grated mature Cheddar cheese
1 teaspoon dried mixed herbs	1 teaspoon dried mixed herbs
1 small onion, grated	1 small onion, grated
1 egg yolk	1 egg yolk

For coating:

Imperial (Metric)	American
1 oz (25g) wholemeal breadcrumbs	½ cup wholewheat breadcrumbs
1 oz (25g) grated Parmesan cheese	¼ cup grated Parmesan cheese
1 egg white, lightly beaten	1 egg white, lightly beaten
Oil for frying	Oil for frying

1. Mix together all the ingredients for the sausages. Divide into twelve pieces and squeeze into sausage shapes.

2. To coat, mix the breadcrumbs and Parmesan. Dip each sausage into the egg white and then into the crumbs.

3. Fry in a little oil for 2-3 minutes on each side.

For a baby:
Mix all the ingredients except the dried herbs together, remove a small portion, and then add the herbs and proceed as above. Omit Parmesan from coating crumbs for a baby too. To spice up the sausages for adults, add ½ teaspoon mustard powder to the adults' portion, or to the crumbs and cheese used to coat their sausages.

Macaroni Cheese de Luxe (serves 4) 2

Imperial (Metric)
4 oz (100g) wholemeal
  macaroni
2 oz (50g) vegetable
  margarine
2 oz (50g) wholemeal flour
1 teaspoon mustard powder
¾ pint (375ml) milk
4 oz (100g) strong cheese,
  grated
1 medium onion, sliced

American
1 cup wholewheat macaroni
¼ cup vegetable margarine
½ cup wholewheat flour
1 teaspoon mustard powder
2 cups milk
1 cup grated strong cheese
1 medium onion, sliced

1. Bring a large saucepanful of water to the boil, add the macaroni and boil for eight minutes. Drain well.

2. Melt half the margarine in another pan and fry the onion for 5 minutes. Add the rest of the margarine, stir in the flour and mustard, and gradually add the milk, stirring all the time.

3. Stir in half the cheese, and add the macaroni. Top with the rest of the cheese and brown under a hot grill. Or prepare in advance and then heat through in an ovenproof dish for 20 minutes at 400°F/200°C (Gas Mark 6).

To vary:
Add one or more of the following: chopped hard-boiled egg, sliced peeled tomatoes, baked beans, or use half tomato juice and half milk instead of all milk.

Cheese Croquettes (serves 4) V2

Imperial (Metric)	American
1½ oz (40g) vegetable margarine	3 tablespoons vegetable margarine
1½ oz (40g) wholemeal flour	⅓ cup wholewheat flour
½ pint (250ml) milk	1¼ cups milk
6 oz (150g) cheese, grated	1½ cups cheese, grated
1 teaspoon mustard powder	1 teaspoon mustard powder
1 teaspoon dried mixed herbs	1 teaspoon dried mixed herbs

To coat:

Imperial (Metric)	American
1 oz (25g) wholemeal flour	¼ cup wholewheat flour
1 egg, beaten	1 egg, beaten
2 oz (50g) dried wholemeal breadcrumbs	½ cup dried wholewheat breadcrumbs
Oil for frying	Oil for frying

1. Put the margarine, flour and milk into a pan, and whisk over a low heat until the margarine has melted and mixture is boiling. Stir with a spoon for 2-3 minutes until thick. Add the cheese, mustard and herbs.

2. Divide the mixture into eight and chill in the fridge for 30 minutes. Form into sausages or cakes, and coat with flour, egg, and crumbs.

3. Fry in a little hot oil for 2-3 minutes on each side until golden. These croquettes will freeze either before or after cooking. If freezing before cooking, they can be cooked from frozen but will need 4-5 minutes per side. They are good served cold too.

For a baby:
Remove the baby's portion before adding the mustard powder and herbs, then proceed as above.

Curd Cheese

A good way to use up any milk which goes off. Just leave it standing in a bowl in a warm place until it goes really thick. Strain through muslin, and leave hanging overnight, or for a shorter length of time, depending on the consistency required. Use as it is, or flavour with herbs or crushed garlic.

Home-made Custard
(makes ½-¾ pint/250-375ml/1¼-2 cups) V2

Much more nutritious and tasty than the bought variety, and it is quick and easy to make. It can be mixed with sweet or savoury foods for a baby.

Imperial (Metric)	American
½ pint (250ml) milk	*1¼ cups milk*
2 tablespoons Demerara sugar (optional)	*2 tablespoons Demerara sugar (optional)*
2 eggs, beaten	*2 eggs, beaten*
A few drops natural vanilla essence (optional)	*A few drops natural vanilla essence (optional)*

1. Put the milk, and sugar if used, in a pan and bring just to the boil. Remove from the heat at once, and pour on to the eggs, stirring.

2. Strain through a sieve back into the pan, and stir over a very gentle heat for about five minutes, until slightly thick. Remove from the heat at once. If the custard curdles through overheating, liquidize it to remove the lumps.

3. Add the vanilla essence. Serve hot or cold.

Home-made Yogurt V2

Imperial (Metric)
1 pint (500ml) milk, whole
or skimmed
2 tablespoons natural yogurt
3 tablespoons dried milk
powder

American
2½ cups milk, whole or
skimmed
2 tablespoons natural yogurt
3 tablespoons dried milk
powder

1. Bring the milk to the boil and allow to simmer gently for 5 minutes. Allow to cool to 110°F/43°C. If you are using long-life milk, or reconstituted milk powder there is no need to boil it first, simply heat to the required temperature.

2. Mix together the yogurt and milk powder. Add a little of the milk, stir well, and gradually pour on the rest of the milk, stirring. Transfer to an electric yogurt maker, or a wide-necked vacuum flask.

3. Leave for about 4 hours at room temperature, or until the yogurt is thick and set. Refrigerate as soon as it is ready, since if it is left too long it will taste acid.

Serve natural yogurt with fresh fruit or instead of cream, or try the following flavourings:

- Cooking apples, stewed with a little honey, a few raisins and a pinch of cinnamon.
- Fresh grapefruit, chopped and mixed with raisins that have been soaked in a little boiling water, and a teaspoonful of honey.
- Dried apricots, chopped, and left to stand in the yogurt for 2-3 hours before serving.
- Equal quantities of yogurt and lightly sweetened strawberry purée.
- Chopped dates, lightly mixed with the yogurt, together with a teaspoonful of honey and a few blanched almonds.

For a savoury yogurt try the following:

- Two tomatoes, chopped and added to ¼ pint (125ml/⅔ cup) natural yogurt, with a little tomato purée (paste) and chopped chives.
- Cucumber, diced and mixed with a little chopped mint.
- Any kind of blue cheese, crumbled, and mixed with chopped chives.

Cheese Soufflé (serves 4) V2

Imperial (Metric)
1½ oz (40g) vegetable
  margarine
3 tablespoons wholemeal
  flour
½ pint (250ml) milk
4 large eggs, separated
3 oz (75g) strong cheese,
  grated
1 teaspoon Dijon mustard
1 tablespoon dried
  wholemeal breadcrumbs
1 tablespoon Parmesan
  cheese

American
3 tablespoons vegetable
  margarine
3 tablespoons wholewheat
  flour
1¼ cups milk
4 large eggs, separated
¾ cup grated strong cheese
1 teaspoon Dijon mustard
1 tablespoon dried
  wholewheat breadcrumbs
1 tablespoon Parmesan
  cheese

1. Preheat the oven to 375°F/190°C (Gas Mark 5). Put the margarine, flour and milk in a pan, and whisk over a low heat until margarine melts and mixture comes to a boil. Stir well over a low heat for 2-3 minutes.

2. Remove from the heat and beat in the egg yolks one at a time. Add the grated cheese and mustard. The soufflé can be prepared in advance to this stage.

3. Whisk the egg whites until stiff but not dry. Fold into the sauce with a metal spoon. Grease a 2½ pint (1.4 litres) soufflé dish generously, and sprinkle with crumbs and Parmesan. Pour in soufflé and bake for 25-30 minutes until well risen and golden. Serve at once.

For a baby:
If you want to omit mustard for your baby, remove a small portion of egg mixture, add a spoonful of egg white, and cook separately in a ramekin dish for about 15 minutes.

Pulses

Butterbean Soup (serves 3-4) V2

Imperial (Metric)	American
4 oz (100g) butter beans, soaked overnight	½ cup Lima beans, soaked overnight
1 oz (25g) butter	2½ tablespoons butter
1 carrot, chopped	1 carrot, chopped
1 medium onion, sliced	1 medium onion, sliced
1 stick celery, chopped	1 stalk celery, chopped
1 medium potato, chopped	1 medium potato, chopped
1½ pints (750ml) stock	3¾ cups stock
1 bay leaf	1 bay leaf
1 rounded tablespoon tomato purée	1 rounded tablespoon tomato paste

1. Fry the onion in the butter for 5 minutes. Add the other vegetables and fry for 2-3 minutes.

2. Add the drained beans, the stock, bay leaf and tomato purée (paste). Cover and simmer for 1 hour (or 20 minutes in a pressure cooker). Remove the bay leaf. Liquidize. This soup freezes very successfully.

Lentil Lasagne (serves 6) V2

Imperial (Metric)
2 tablespoons oil
2 onions, sliced
1 large clove garlic, crushed
4 oz (100g) carrots, finely
   chopped
2 sticks celery, chopped
14 oz (400g) tin tomatoes
2 tablespoons tomato purée
½ teaspoon oregano
1 tablespoon chopped
   parsley
12 oz (350g) wholemeal
   noodles
4 oz (100g) brown lentils
Bouquet garni

American
2 tablespoons oil
2 onions, sliced
1 large clove garlic, crushed
⅔ cup finely chopped
   carrots
2 stalks celery, chopped
14 ounce can tomatoes
2 tablespoons tomato paste
½ teaspoon oregano
1 tablespoon chopped
   parsley
3 cups wholewheat noodles
½ cup brown lentils
Bouquet garni

For topping:

Imperial (Metric)
2 eggs, beaten
½ pint (250ml) natural
   yogurt
1 oz (25g) Parmesan cheese

American
2 eggs, beaten
1¼ cups plain yogurt
¼ cup Parmesan cheese

1. Fry the onion, garlic, carrots and celery in the oil for 5 minutes.
   Add the tomatoes, tomato purée (paste), oregano and parsley
   and cook for about 30 minutes until thick.

2. Cook the noodles in plenty of boiling water for 8 minutes,
   drain.

3. Cook the lentils in boiling water with the bouquet garni for
   50 minutes, or until tender. Drain, remove the bouquet garni,
   and add lentils to the vegetables. Mash or purée.

4. In a shallow baking dish or roasting tin put layers of lentil sauce, and noodles, ending with the sauce.

5. Beat together the topping ingredients, pour over, and bake at 400°F/200°C (Gas Mark 6) for 50 minutes.

Home-Baked Beans (serves 4) V2

The taste of home-baked beans is enough to put you off the tinned variety for life! This recipe can be served either as a main course, perhaps topped with cheese or served with jacket potatoes, or as an accompaniment.

Imperial (Metric)	American
8 oz (250g) haricot beans, soaked overnight	1 cup navy beans, soaked overnight
1 large onion, sliced	1 large onion, sliced
1 tablespoon oil	1 tablespoon oil
1 teaspoon mustard powder	1 teaspoon mustard powder
2 teaspoons molasses	2 teaspoons molasses
2 tablespoons tomato purée	2 tablespoons tomato paste
2 teaspoons Muscovado sugar	2 teaspoons Muscovado sugar
¾ pint (375ml) stock	2 cups stock
2 tablespoons cider vinegar	2 tablespoons cider vinegar

1.   Drain the beans. Cook in boiling water for about an hour (or 15 minutes in a pressure cooker) until almost tender.

2.   Fry the onion in the oil for 5 minutes, add the rest of the ingredients and the drained beans, and bring to the boil.

3.   Cover and cook at 275°F/140°C (Gas Mark 1) for 4 hours, stirring occasionally. This recipe freezes well.

Hummus (serves 4 as a snack, or 2 as a meal) V2

This delicious chick pea (garbanzo) and sesame dish, which is eaten throughout the Middle East, makes a lovely spread or dip, a starter or even a salad meal if pressed into a lightly oiled mould and then turned out on to a plate.

Imperial (Metric)	American
4 oz (100g) chick peas, soaked overnight	½ cup garbanzo beans, soaked overnight
1 clove garlic, crushed	1 clove garlic, crushed
Juice of 1 lemon	Juice of 1 lemon
2 tablespoons tahini (see page 44)	2 tablespoons tahini (see page 44)
4 tablespoons olive oil	4 tablespoons olive oil
2 tablespoons lightly toasted sesame seeds (optional)	2 tablespoons lightly toasted sesame seeds (optional)
Freshly ground black pepper	Freshly ground black pepper

1. Drain the chick peas (garbanzos), and cook in plenty of boiling water for about an hour (20 minutes in a pressure cooker), or until quite tender.

2. Drain, and put into a blender with the other ingredients. Liquidize until smooth, adding a little of the cooking liquid if necessary, and pushing the mixture down on to the blades. Chill or freeze.

For a baby:
Omit the sesame seeds until your baby is old enough to cope with them.

Normandy Beans (serves 4)

Imperial (Metric)	American
4 oz (100g) haricot beans, soaked overnight	½ cup navy beans, soaked overnight
1 large onion, sliced	1 large onion, sliced
2 tablespoons oil	2 tablespoons oil
12 oz (350g) potatoes, diced	12 ounces potatoes, diced
¼ pint (125ml) dry cider	⅔ cup dry cider
½ pint (250ml) stock or water	1¼ cups stock or water
½ teaspoon oregano	½ teaspoon oregano
12 oz (350g) cooking apples	12 ounces cooking apples
1 tablespoon chopped parsley	1 tablespoon chopped parsley

1. Drain the beans and cook in boiling water until tender (about 1 hour, or 20 minutes in a pressure cooker). Drain.

2. Fry the onion in oil for 5 minutes. Add the potatoes, oregano and liquid and simmer for 15 minutes.

3. Peel, core and slice apples and add with beans. Cook for a further 10 minutes. Garnish with parsley and serve.

Grains and Nuts

Rice and Cheese Croquettes (serves 4) V2

Imperial (Metric)
8 oz (250g) cold cooked
  brown rice
4 oz (100g) grated cheese
1 egg, beaten
1 small onion, grated
1 tablespoon chopped
  parsley
1 tablespoon wholemeal
  flour

American
1 cup cold cooked brown
  rice
1 cup grated cheese
1 egg, beaten
1 small onion, grated
1 tablespoon chopped
  parsley
1 tablespoon wholewheat
  flour

To coat:

Imperial (Metric)
1 egg, beaten
2 oz (50g) dried wholemeal
  breadcrumbs

American
1 egg, beaten
½ cup dried wholewheat
  breadcrumbs

Oil for frying

Oil for frying

1. Mix together all the croquette ingredients. Divide into eight portions, and squeeze into cake shapes.

2. Coat with the crumbs, pressing in well. The mixture is fairly sticky and crumbly, so handle with care.

3. Fry for 2-3 minutes on each side or until golden-brown. To vary, use other cooked grains in place of the rice.

Barley Stew (serves 4) V2

Imperial (Metric)	American
1 onion, sliced	1 onion, sliced
1 clove garlic, crushed	1 clove garlic, crushed
2 sticks celery, chopped	2 stalks celery, chopped
2 carrots, sliced	2 carrots, sliced
2 tablespoons oil	2 tablespoons oil
12 oz (350g) pot barley	1½ cups pot barley
14 oz (400g) tin tomatoes	14 ounce can tomatoes
½ pint (250ml) stock	1¼ cups stock
1 bay leaf	1 bay leaf
1 teaspoon dried mixed herbs	1 teaspoon dried mixed herbs
4 oz (100g) mushrooms, sliced	1 cup mushrooms, sliced
1 tablespoon chopped parsley	1 tablespoon chopped parsley
1 tablespoon soya sauce	1 tablespoon soy sauce

1. Fry the chopped vegetables in the oil for 5 minutes. Add the barley and cook for a further 5 minutes, stirring.

2. Pour on the tomatoes and stock, add the herbs and simmer for 50 minutes, or until barley is tender, adding more liquid if necessary. Ten minutes before the end add the sliced mushrooms and stir in the soya sauce.

3. Garnish with parsley before serving. To vary, use other wholegrains in place of the barley.

For a baby:
Cook a portion without herbs, mushrooms or soya sauce.

Bulgur Wheat Pilaf (serves 4) V2

Imperial (Metric)	American
8 oz (250g) bulgur wheat	1½ cups bulgur wheat
1 pint (500ml) boiling water	2½ cups boiling water
3 tablespoons oil	3 tablespoons oil
2 large onions, sliced	2 large onions, sliced
1 clove garlic, crushed	1 clove garlic, crushed
2 sticks celery, chopped	2 stalks celery, chopped
1 carrot, grated	1 carrot, grated
2 oz (50g) raisins	⅓ cup raisins
4 oz (100g) almonds, lightly toasted	¾ cup almonds, lightly toasted

1. Soak the bulgur in the boiling water for 20 minutes.

2. Meanwhile, fry the onions, garlic and celery in the oil for 5 minutes. Add the carrot, the drained bulgur, and the raisins.

3. Cook for 5 minutes, then cover and cook very gently for a further 10 minutes. Sprinkle the nuts on before serving. If you want to prepare this in advance, heat through at 350°F/180°C (Gas Mark 4) for 30 minutes, but do not add the nuts until ready to serve.

For a baby:
Omit the nuts.

Saucy Nut Roast (serves 4) V

Imperial (Metric)
2 tablespoons oil
1 onion, finely chopped
1 clove of garlic, crushed
2 sticks celery, finely chopped
1 tablespoon wholemeal flour
⅔ pint (350ml) V8 vegetable juice
4 oz (100g) fresh wholemeal breadcrumbs
4 oz (100g) hazelnuts or peanuts, coarsely ground
1 tablespoon porridge oats
1 tablespoon chopped parsley
1 egg, beaten

American
2 tablespoons oil
1 onion, finely chopped
1 clove of garlic, crushed
2 stalks celery, finely chopped
1 tablespoon wholewheat flour
1½ cups V8 vegetable juice
2 cups fresh wholewheat breadcrumbs
¾ cup coarsely ground hazelnuts or peanuts
1 tablespoon rolled oats
1 tablespoon chopped parsley
1 egg, beaten

For the sauce:

Imperial (Metric)
1 tablespoon wholemeal flour
1 tablespoon vegetable margarine
½ teaspoon dried basil

American
1 tablespoon wholewheat flour
1 tablespoon vegetable margarine
½ teaspoon dried basil

1. Fry the onion, garlic and celery in the oil for 5 minutes. Add the flour, stirring, and cook for 2 minutes. Gradually stir in half the vegetable juice. Reserve the remaining juice for the sauce.

2. Add the rest of the ingredients, mix well, and press into a greased 7 inch (20cm) square cake tin. Cover with foil and bake at 350°F/180°C (Gas Mark 4) for 45 minutes. Remove the foil and bake for a further 15 minutes.

3. Meanwhile, make a sauce with the margarine, flour and the rest of the vegetable juice, adding a little milk if necessary. Stir in the basil.

Risotto (serves 4) V2

Imperial (Metric)	American
2 tablespoons oil	2 tablespoons oil
1 large onion, sliced	1 large onion, sliced
1 clove garlic, crushed	1 clove garlic, crushed
2 carrots, diced	2 carrots, diced
8 oz (250g) brown rice	1 cup brown rice
½ pint (250ml) water or stock	1¼ cups water or stock
1 lb (500g) tomatoes, peeled and chopped	1 pound tomatoes, peeled and chopped
2 tablespoons chopped parsley	2 tablespoons chopped parsley
2 oz (50g) cottage cheese	¼ cup cottage cheese
2 oz (50g) grated cheese	½ cup grated cheese
2 oz (50g) toasted almonds	½ cup toasted almonds

1. Fry the vegetables in the oil for 5 minutes. Add the rice and stir well to coat with oil.

2. Add the water or stock and the tomatoes and cook, uncovered, for about an hour, adding extra liquid if necessary. The mixture should be soft but not liquid.

3. Before serving stir in the nuts and parsley. Spread the cottage cheese over the risotto, and sprinkle on the grated cheese. Put a lid on the pan for a further 5 minutes to melt the cheeses slightly.

There are endless variations on risotto: try using different vegetables; or add cooked chopped meat and meat stock; or omit the tomatoes and add prawns and toasted flaked almonds.

For a baby:
Omit the nuts.

Vegetable Dishes and Accompaniments

Mixed Vegetable Soup (serves 4) V2

Imperial (Metric)	American
1 large potato, chopped but not peeled	1 large potato, chopped but not peeled
2 large carrots, sliced	2 large carrots, sliced
1 large onion, sliced	1 large onion, sliced
2 celery sticks, chopped	2 celery stalks, chopped
1 oz (25g) butter	2½ tablespoons butter
2 pints (1 litre) well-flavoured vegetable stock	5 cups well-flavoured vegetable stock
Small bunch parsley	Small bunch parsley
1 bay leaf	1 bay leaf
Sprig of fresh thyme	Sprig of fresh thyme
¼ pint (125ml) milk	⅔ cup milk
2 tablespoons wholemeal flour	2 tablespoons wholewheat flour

1. Fry the vegetables in the butter for five minutes. Add the stock. Tie together the herbs with a piece of thread and add. Simmer for 50 minutes (or 15 minutes in a pressure cooker). Blend until smooth.

2. Whisk together the flour and the milk. Add to the soup, stirring, and bring to the boil. Cook for 2-3 minutes until thick.

The flavour of this soup can be altered by using different vegetables in season. It freezes well.

Sweetcorn and Potato Soup (serves 4-6) V2

Imperial (Metric)	American
1 oz (25g) butter or margarine	2½ tablespoons butter or margarine
1 medium onion, sliced	1 medium onion, sliced
1 green pepper, deseeded and chopped	1 green pepper, deseeded and chopped
1 tablespoon wholemeal flour	1 tablespoon wholewheat flour
2 medium potatoes, boiled for 10 minutes, drained and diced	2 medium potatoes, boiled for 10 minutes, drained and diced
10 oz (285g) frozen sweetcorn	1⅔ cups frozen sweetcorn
½ pint (250ml) vegetable stock	1¼ cups vegetable stock
½ pint (250ml) milk	1¼ cups milk
4 oz (100g) mushrooms, sliced	2 cups mushrooms, sliced

1. Melt the butter or margarine and fry the onions and pepper for 5 minutes. Stir in the flour, cook for 2-3 minutes, then gradually pour on the stock and milk.

2. Add the potatoes, sweetcorn and mushrooms. Cover, and simmer gently for 15-20 minutes.

For a baby:
You could purée a small portion of the soup, omitting the green pepper or mushrooms if you find they disagree with your baby.

Sweetcorn Fritters (serves 4-6 as an accompaniment) V2

Imperial (Metric)	American
4 oz (100g) wholemeal flour	1 cup wholewheat flour
1 egg, beaten	1 egg, beaten
¼ pint (125ml) milk	⅔ cup milk
8 oz (250g) frozen sweetcorn, thawed, or 12 oz (340g) tin, drained	1⅓ cups sweetcorn kernels, thawed if frozen
Oil for frying	Oil for frying

1. Put the flour in a bowl, add the egg and half the milk, and beat until smooth. Gradually add the rest of the milk, beating well. Stir in the sweetcorn.

2. Heat a little oil in a large frying pan. Drop spoonsful of batter into the pan, and cook for 3-4 minutes on each side, until golden brown. Serve at once.

To vary:
This recipe can also be used for other cooked vegetables, for chopped nuts, chopped diced meat, cooked pulses, or any other leftovers you have to hand.

Carrots with Raisins (serves 4) V2

Imperial (Metric)
8-12 oz (250-350g) carrots
1 oz (25g) butter
2 tablespoons stock
1 tablespoon raisins, soaked
  in a little boiling water
1 tablespoon chopped
  parsley

American
8-12 ounces carrots
2½ tablespoons butter
2 tablespoons stock
1 tablespoon raisins, soaked
  in a little boiling water
1 tablespoon chopped
  parsley

1. Scrub the carrots and slice into strips, about 2 inches × ⅛ inch (50cm×3mm).

2. Put into a pan of cold water, bring to the boil, and drain at once, reserving the liquid for other uses.

3. Melt the butter, and add all the other ingredients except the parsley. Cover and cook over a low heat for 10-15 minutes, shaking occasionally. Garnish with parsley and serve at once.

Stuffed Baked Potatoes (serves 4)

1. Bake 4 medium-sized old potatoes at 400°F/200°C (Gas Mark 6), for about 1 hour, or until cooked through (test with a fork).

Peanut Butter and Ham

Imperial (Metric)
8 oz (250g) lean ham,
    chopped
4 oz (100g) peanut butter
1 oz (25g) butter

American
8 ounces lean ham, chopped
½ cup peanut butter
2½ tablespoons butter

1. Mix together the ham and peanut butter. Cut the potatoes in half, add a knob of butter, and stuff with the filling ingredients. Return to the oven for 10 minutes to warm through.

Tuna and Sour Cream

Imperial (Metric)	American
7 oz (190g) tin tuna in brine	7 ounce can tuna in brine
¼ pint (125ml) sour cream	⅔ cup soured cream
2 tablespoons chopped parsley	2 tablespoons chopped parsley
2 oz (50g) grated cheese	½ cup grated cheese

1. Mix together the drained tuna, the cream and the parsley. Cut the cooked potatoes in half, scoop out most of the insides of the potatoes, and mash roughly with a fork.

2. Mix together the stuffing and the potato, and pile back into the potato cases. Scatter over the grated cheese, and return to the oven for 15 minutes or until the cheese has melted and browned.

Almond and Cheese

Imperial (Metric)
4 tablespoons flaked
  almonds
2 tablespoons cream
2 tablespoons natural yogurt
5 tablespoons grated cheese
1 tablespoon Parmesan
  cheese

American
4 tablespoons slivered
  almonds
2 tablespoons cream
2 tablespoons plain yogurt
5 tablespoons grated cheese
1 tablespoon Parmesan
  cheese

1. Fry the nuts in a little oil or butter until golden. Heat the grill
    (broiler) to high.

2. Remove a slice from the top of each potato, and carefully
    scoop out the middle. Mash and mix with the almonds, cream
    and yogurt.

3. Pile back into the potatoes and top with the two cheeses.
    Put under the hot grill until the cheese has melted and
    browned.

Beansprouts V2

Beansprouts are cheap and easy to grow at home, and provide a highly nutritious food which is readily available all year round. Sprouts are rich in vitamins C, A, E, K, B_2, B_6 and folic acid, as well as the minerals calcium, iron and magnesium.

Alfalfa is a good one to start with, since it is not only the most nutritious but also the best liked, being similar in taste to cress. Other varieties you can try are mung beans (traditionally used in Chinese food), lentils, wheat, oats, soya beans, and chick peas (garbanzos).

To grow your own sprouts, soak a tablespoon of grains or pulses in warm water for several hours. Drain well (keep the liquid for cooking), and put into a glass jar. Cover the top with muslin, or pierce holes in the lid to allow the air to circulate. Leave in a warm room, and rinse the sprouts twice a day with warm water, draining well each time.

The sprouts will take anything up to five days to grow big enough to eat. Wheat and other grains are ready when the sprout is about ½ inch (1cm) long; lentils 1 inch (2.5cm); mung, soya and chick peas 1½-2 inches (4-5cm); and alfalfa 1½ inches (4cm). Sprouts are best if grown in the light, because although they will be shorter, they will also be richer in vitamin C, protein and trace elements than if they were grown in the dark. They will also look greener, too, since chlorophyll is only formed where there is exposure to light.

Once your sprouts are ready, they will keep in the fridge for several days. Use them in salads, or sandwiches, or add them during the last few minutes of cooking time to such dishes as risottos, soups, rissoles or quiches.

Salads and Salad Dressings

As explained in the section on diet (page 15), eating fresh raw fruit and vegetables is an integral part of a wholefood diet. Because of this salads should be eaten all the year round, and should be far more adventurous than the traditional lettuce, tomato and cucumber. In the winter months, for instance, try including such vegetables as raw cauliflower, leeks, mushrooms, young Brussels sprouts, grated beetroot — the possibilities are endless.

One of the easiest ways to introduce variety is to make an 'anything goes' salad, where you combine a selection of whatever vegetables you have to hand. Liven up the salad with fresh or dried fruit, nuts, cubes of cheese etc., and with no effort at all you can have a different salad for every day of the week. Add a different dressing, and even the same salad ingredients can take on a new taste.

Some of the recipes that follow are suitable as the basis of a main course, simply needing the addition of rice, potatoes or bread, while others are intended to be served as an accompaniment.

Tuna Waldorf Salad (serves 4 as a main course)

Imperial (Metric)
7 oz (190g) tin tuna in brine
4 sticks celery
2 oz (50g) walnuts
2 dessert apples
Juice of ½ lemon
¼-½ pint (125-250ml)
mayonnaise

American
7 ounce can tuna in brine
4 stalks celery
½ cup English walnuts
2 dessert apples
Juice of ½ lemon
⅔ to 1¼ cups mayonnaise

1. Drain and flake the tuna. Chop the celery and nuts and add to the tuna. Core but do not peel the apples. Dice and toss in the lemon juice.

2. Add the apple cubes to the tuna and stir in sufficient mayonnaise to bind. Serve with lettuce or watercress.

Carrots and Apple Vinaigrette (serves 4) V2

Imperial (Metric)
2 large carrots
2 dessert apples
2 tablespoons sunflower
  seeds
2 tablespoons raisins
2 tablespoons French
  dressing
1 tablespoon chopped
  parsley

American
2 large carrots
2 dessert apples
2 tablespoons sunflower
  seeds
2 tablespoons raisins
2 tablespoons French
  dressing
1 tablespoon chopped
  parsley

1. Grate the carrots and the apples, and mix together with the other ingredients, adding enough dressing to moisten.

2. Garnish with chopped parsley. To vary substitute mayonnaise for the dressing.

For a baby:
If preferred, omit the sunflower seeds and the dressing.

Peanut Apple and Celery Salad (serves 4) V2

Imperial (Metric)	American
2 dessert apples	2 dessert apples
3 sticks celery	3 stalks celery
2 oz (50g) salted peanuts	½ cup salted peanuts
2 spring onions (optional)	2 scallions (optional)
1 tablespoon runny honey	1 tablespoon runny honey
1 tablespoon lemon juice	1 tablespoon lemon juice

1. Chop the apples, celery and spring onions (scallions) if used. Add the peanuts.

2. Mix together the honey and lemon juice and pour over the vegetables.

For a baby:
Omit the peanuts for young children, because they may cause choking.

Chicken and Banana Salad (serves 4) 2

Imperial (Metric)	American
¼ pint (125ml) natural yogurt	⅔ cup plain yogurt
½ tablespoon tomato purée	½ tablespoon tomato paste
12 oz (350g) cooked chicken, chopped	12 ounces cooked chicken, chopped
2 large bananas, sliced	2 large bananas, sliced
2 oz (50g) flaked almonds	½ cup slivered almonds

1. Mix together the yogurt and tomato purée (paste). Stir in the chicken and banana and leave to stand for at least an hour for the flavour to develop.

2. Lightly toast the almonds under a medium grill (broiler), and scatter over the salad just before serving.

For a baby:
Serve without the nuts.

Brown Rice Salad (serves 4 as a main course, 6-8 as an accompaniment) V2

Imperial (Metric)
8 oz (250g) brown rice
1 pint (500ml) boiling water
2 teaspoons oil
2-3 tablespoons French dressing
2 spring onions, finely chopped
2 oz (50g) currants or raisins
¼ small cucumber, diced
2 dessert apples, unpeeled but chopped
3 tomatoes, peeled and chopped
2 oz (50g) almonds

American
1 cup brown rice
2½ cups boiling water
2 teaspoons oil
2-3 tablespoons French dressing
2 scallions, finely chopped
⅓ cup currants or raisins
¼ small cucumber, diced
2 dessert apples, unpeeled but chopped
3 tomatoes, peeled and chopped
½ cup almonds

1. Heat the oil in a pan, add the rice and stir well. Pour on the water, stir once, cover and simmer for about 40 minutes until rice is cooked and water is absorbed. Tip rice into a bowl, fluff up with a fork, and pour on dressing. Leave until cold.

2. Mix in the other ingredients except the almonds. Before serving lightly toast the almonds under a medium grill (broiler) and stir into the rice.

For a baby:
Omit the almonds, and the dressing if preferred.

Banana Salad (serves 4) V2

Imperial (Metric)
1 large carrot, grated
3 inch (7cm) piece
   cucumber, diced
3 oz (75g) dried apricots,
   chopped
½ banana, sliced
1 tablespoon sunflower
   seeds

American
1 large carrot, grated
3 inch piece cucumber,
   diced
½ cup dried apricots,
   chopped
½ banana, sliced
1 tablespoon sunflower
   seeds

For the dressing:

Imperial (Metric)
2 tablespoons mayonnaise
½ banana, mashed
1 tablespoon natural yogurt

American
2 tablespoons mayonnaise
½ banana, mashed
1 tablespoon plain yogurt

1. Combine all the salad ingredients in a bowl.

2. To make the dressing, mix the ingredients together and stir
    into the salad. This dressing is also good served with a
    coleslaw salad.

For a baby:
Omit the seeds if preferred.

Tuna and Bean Salad (serves 4 as a main course) 2

Imperial (Metric)
4 oz (100g) butter beans

American
¾ cup Lima beans

For the dressing:

Imperial (Metric)
1 clove garlic, crushed
3 tablespoons olive oil
1 tablespoon cider vinegar
1 teaspoon Dijon mustard

2 tablespoons finely
   chopped onion
2 tablespoons chopped
   parsley
7 oz (190g) tin tuna in brine
12 black olives (optional)

American
1 clove garlic, crushed
3 tablespoons olive oil
1 tablespoon cider vinegar
1 teaspoon Dijon mustard

2 tablespoons finely
   chopped onion
2 tablespoons chopped
   parsley
7 ounce can tuna in brine
12 black olives (optional)

1. Soak the beans overnight and cook in boiling water until
   tender (about 1 hour, or 20 minutes in a pressure cooker).
   Drain. Mix the dressing ingredients in a screwtop jar and add
   while the beans are still hot. Allow to cool and stir in onion
   and parsley. Leave to stand for at least an hour.

2. Drain and flake the tuna, and mix gently into beans. Top with
   olives if used, and serve with lettuce and wholemeal pitta
   bread.

For a baby:
Serve without the onion, olives or dressing.

Wholemeal Pasta Salad (serves 4) V

Imperial (Metric)
4 oz (100g) wholemeal
  macaroni or pasta shells
4 tablespoons mayonnaise
2 tablespoons natural yogurt
4 spring onions, chopped
4 tomatoes, peeled and
  chopped
4 oz (100g) cooked
  sweetcorn
Bunch of watercress

American
1 cup wholewheat macaroni
  or pasta shells
4 tablespoons mayonnaise
2 tablespoons plain yogurt
4 scallions, chopped
4 tomatoes, peeled and
  chopped
⅔ cup cooked sweetcorn
Bunch of watercress

1.   Cook the pasta in plenty of boiling water for 8 minutes. Drain
     well. Mix together the mayonnaise and yogurt and stir into
     the pasta while still hot.

2.   When pasta is cold add the rest of the ingredients, and serve
     garnished with watercress.

French Dressing (makes about ½ pint/ 250ml/1¼ cups)

Imperial (Metric)
Juice of 1 lemon
2 tablespoons cider vinegar
⅓ pint (200ml) olive oil
¼ teaspoon freshly ground
  black pepper
½ teaspoon sea salt
1 teaspoon French mustard

American
Juice of 1 lemon
2 tablespoons cider vinegar
¾ cup olive oil
¼ teaspoon freshly ground
  black pepper
½ teaspoon sea salt
1 teaspoon French mustard

1. Put all the ingredients into a screw-topped jar, put on the lid and shake thoroughly.

2. Store in a cool place, and shake well before use.

Note: Although both these dressing recipes specify olive oil, I find that sunflower oil (which is considerably cheaper, and higher in polyunsaturates) is an acceptable alternative.

Mayonnaise (makes about ½ pint/ 250ml/1¼ cups)

Imperial (Metric)
1 egg
½ teaspoon sea salt
½ teaspoon French mustard
2 teaspoons cider vinegar
½ pint (250ml) olive oil

American
1 egg
½ teaspoon sea salt
½ teaspoon French mustard
2 teaspoons cider vinegar
1¼ cups olive oil

1. Put the egg, salt, mustard and vinegar into a blender and blend for a few seconds. Add the oil very slowly through the hole in the lid, and continue to add until the mayonnaise thickens.

2. To make by hand, add the oil drop by drop, whisking or beating until half has been added. Continue to add gradually until all the oil has been used.

Meat

Mince and Rice Bake (serves 4) 2

Imperial (Metric)
1 onion, sliced
2 tablespoons oil
1 lb (500g) minced beef
14 oz (400g) tin tomatoes,
  puréed
3 oz (75g) raisins
4 oz (100g) long grain brown
  rice
2 oz (50g) beansprouts

American
1 onion, sliced
2 tablespoons oil
2 cups ground beef
14 oz can tomatoes
  puréed
½ cup raisins
½ cup long grain brown rice
1 cup beansprouts

Topping:

Imperial (Metric)
2 eggs, beaten
¼ pint (125ml) natural
  yogurt
3 oz (75g) grated cheddar
  cheese

American
2 eggs, beaten
⅔ cup plain yogurt
¾ cup grated cheddar
  cheese

1. Fry onion in the oil for 5 minutes. Add the mince and brown. Add the tomatoes, raisins and rice. Cover and cook for 30 minutes, adding a little water if necessary.

2. Stir in the beansprouts. Put in an ovenproof dish. Mix together the yogurt and eggs and pour over. Scatter the cheese over the top. Heat the oven to 400°F/200°C (Gas Mark 6), and bake at the top of the oven for 20-25 minutes.

Chicken with Peanut Butter Sauce (serves 4)

Imperial (Metric)
4 chicken pieces, skinned
2 tablespoons oil
1 tablespoon wholemeal
  flour
3 tablespoons peanut butter
¾ pint (375ml) chicken
  stock
2 teaspoons lemon juice
1 oz (25g) salted peanuts

American
4 chicken pieces, skinned
2 tablespoons oil
1 tablespoon wholewheat
  flour
3 tablespoons peanut butter
2 cups chicken stock
2 teaspoons lemon juice
¼ cup salted peanuts

1. Fry the chicken in the oil for 5 minutes on each side.

2. Mix together the flour and peanut butter and add to the pan.
   Gradually add the stock and lemon juice. Cover and simmer
   for at least 15 minutes.

3. A few minutes before serving stir in the salted peanuts.

Beef and Nut Loaf (serves 4)

Imperial (Metric)	American
2 onions, sliced	2 onions, sliced
2 tablespoons oil	2 tablespoons oil
1 teaspoon curry powder	1 teaspoon curry powder
2 teaspoons raw cane sugar	2 teaspoons raw cane sugar
1 teaspoon lemon juice	1 teaspoon lemon juice
1 lb (500g) minced beef	2 cups ground beef
4 oz (100g) wholemeal bread	4 ounces wholewheat bread
1/3 pint (200ml) milk	3/4 cup milk
1 egg yolk	1 egg yolk
1 oz (25g) almonds	1/4 cup almonds

1. Fry the onions in the oil. Stir in the curry powder and sugar, then add the lemon juice and mince. Cook for a few minutes until meat is brown all over.

2. Soak the bread in a little milk for 15 minutes, then mash with a fork and add to the meat. Put in a large greased loaf tin.

3. Blend the yolk with 1/4 pint (125ml, 2/3 cup) of milk, and add the almonds. Pour over the meat and bake for 1 hour at 350°F/180°C (Gas Mark 4).

Liver Casserole (serves 4) 2

Imperial (Metric)	American
1 lb (500g) lamb's liver	1 pound lamb's liver
2 tablespoons wholemeal flour	2 tablespoons wholewheat flour
1 large onion, sliced	1 large onion, sliced
1 green pepper, deseeded and chopped	1 green pepper, deseeded and chopped
2 tablespoons oil	2 tablespoons oil
14 oz (400g) tin tomatoes	14 ounce can tomatoes

1. Cut the liver into even-sized pieces and coat with flour. Fry the onion and the pepper in the oil for 5 minutes.

2. Add the liver and brown quickly. Put in a casserole with the tomatoes. Cover and bake at 350°F/180°C (Gas Mark 4) for 45 minutes.

Mince and Macaroni Bake (serves 4) 2

Imperial (Metric)
1 onion, sliced
1 tablespoon oil
1 clove of garlic, crushed
8 oz (250g) minced beef
2 heaped tablespoons tomato
  purée
8 oz (250g) tinned tomatoes
4 oz (100g) wholemeal
  macaroni
1 oz (25g) vegetable
  margarine
1 oz (25g) wholemeal flour
⅓ pint (200ml) milk
Freshly grated nutmeg
4 oz (100g) grated cheese

American
1 onion, sliced
1 tablespoon oil
1 clove of garlic, crushed
1 cup ground beef
2 heaped tablespoons tomato
  paste
8 ounces canned tomatoes
1 cup wholewheat macaroni
2 tablespoons vegetable
  margarine
¼ cup wholewheat flour
¾ cup milk
Freshly grated nutmeg
1 cup grated cheese

1. Fry the onion in the oil. Add the garlic and the mince, and brown the meat. Stir in the tomato purée (paste) and the tin of tomatoes, and simmer for 15-20 minutes until thick.

2. Boil the macaroni in plenty of water for eight minutes. Drain. Stir into the meat.

3. Make a sauce by whisking together the margarine, flour and milk, continuing to whisk until boiling. Add some freshly grated nutmeg, stir well and simmer for 5 minutes. Stir into the meat.

4. Put in a baking dish, sprinkle cheese over, and bake for 30 minutes at 350°F/180°C (Gas Mark 4).

Chicken Croquettes (serves 4) 2

Imperial (Metric)
3 oz (75g) vegetable
  margarine
1 onion, finely sliced
1 clove of garlic, crushed
4 oz (100g) wholemeal flour
⅔ pint (350ml) milk
Grated rind of 1 lemon
2 tablespoons chopped
  capers (optional)
12 oz (350g) cooked chicken,
  minced
1 tablespoon chopped
  parsley
1 teaspoon dried tarragon

American
⅓ cup vegetable margarine
1 onion, finely sliced
1 clove of garlic, crushed
1 cup wholewheat flour
1½ cups milk
Grated rind of 1 lemon
2 tablespoons chopped
  capers (optional)
12 ounces cooked chicken,
  minced
1 tablespoon chopped
  parsley
1 teaspoon dried tarragon

To coat:

Imperial (Metric)
2 eggs, beaten
2 oz (50g) dried wholemeal
  breadcrumbs
Oil for frying

American
2 eggs, beaten
1 cup dried wholewheat
  breadcrumbs
Oil for frying

1. Melt the margarine and fry the onion and the garlic. Add the flour and cook over a low heat for 2-3 minutes, stirring. Gradually add the milk. Mix in the rest of the ingredients and cool overnight or for several hours.

2. Shape into 12 equal-sized croquette shapes. Dip into the beaten egg and then the crumbs. Fry in a little oil for 2-3 minutes on each side until golden-brown. These croquettes freeze well.

Fish

Tunaburgers (serves 4) 2

These make a delicious alternative to hamburgers, and can be served on their own or inside a wholemeal bun. They can be frozen before cooking, in which case fry them for about 5 minutes on each side.

Imperial (Metric)	American
1 small onion, very finely chopped	1 small onion, very finely chopped
1 stick celery, very finely chopped	1 stalk celery, very finely chopped
2 tablespoons oil	2 tablespoons oil
7 oz (190g) tin tuna in brine	7 ounce can tuna in brine
2 oz (50g) fresh wholemeal breadcrumbs	1 cup fresh wholewheat breadcrumbs
Pinch of chilli seasoning	Pinch of chili seasoning
1 teaspoon lemon juice	1 teaspoon lemon juice
2 tablespoons mayonnaise	2 tablespoons mayonnaise

1. Fry the onion and celery in half the oil for 5 minutes.

2. Drain and flake the tuna into a bowl and mix in all the other ingredients. Divide into four and shape into round cakes.

3. Heat the rest of the oil in a pan, and fry for 2-3 minutes on each side until golden-brown. Serve with lemon wedges if liked.

Sardine Bake (serves 4) 2

Imperial (Metric)	American
3 × 3 ½ oz (85g) tins sardines, drained	3 × 3 ½ ounce cans sardines, drained
Good pinch each of dried tarragon, thyme, basil and oregano	Large pinch each of dried tarragon, thyme, basil and oregano
2 oz (50g) capers, drained and chopped	¼ cup capers, drained and chopped
1 lb (500g) tomatoes	1 pound tomatoes
2 tablespoons oil	2 tablespoons oil
1½ oz (37g) dried wholemeal breadcrumbs	⅓ cup dried wholewheat breadcrumbs
2 tablespoons Parmesan cheese	2 tablespoons Parmesan cheese

1. Lay the sardines in a shallow ovenproof dish and sprinkle over the herbs and capers.

2. Peel and thickly slice the tomatoes and lay over the fish. Sprinkle over the oil, the breadcrumbs and the Parmesan. Bake at 350°F/180°C (Gas Mark 4) for 30 minutes, or until golden-brown.

For a baby:
Omit herbs and capers.

Fish Spaghetti (serves 4)

Imperial (Metric)	American
2 tablespoons oil	2 tablespoons oil
1 onion, sliced	1 onion, sliced
1 clove garlic, crushed	1 clove garlic, crushed
4 juicy tomatoes, peeled and chopped	4 juicy tomatoes, peeled and chopped
½ teaspoon dried basil	½ teaspoon dried basil
7 oz (190g) tin tuna in brine	7 ounce can tuna in brine
1 tablespoon capers, drained and chopped	1 tablespoon capers, drained and chopped
6 oz (150g) wholemeal spaghetti	6 ounces wholewheat spaghetti

1. Fry the onion in the oil for 5 minutes, add the garlic for 2 minutes.

2. Add the rest of the sauce ingredients and cook over a low heat for 15 minutes, adding a little water if necessary.

3. Meanwhile, cook the spaghetti in plenty of boiling water for 12 minutes. Drain well and top with the sauce. Serve at once.

Baked Crumbed Fish (serves 4) 2

Imperial (Metric)	American
1 lb (500g) fresh haddock fillets	1 pound fresh haddock fillets
2 oz (50g) melted butter	¼ cup melted butter
1 egg, beaten	1 egg, beaten
4 oz (100g) dried wholemeal breadcrumbs	1 cup dried wholewheat breadcrumbs

1. Remove the skin from the fish with a sharp knife. Mix the egg and butter. Coat fish with this and then with the breadcrumbs, pressing well into the fish.

2. Place the fish side by side in a shallow dish. Bake at 375°F/190°C (Gas Mark 5) for about 40 minutes. Do not turn.

Sardine and Tomato Flan (serves 4)

Imperial (Metric)
6 oz (150g) wholemeal pastry
2×3½ oz (85g) tins sardines
   in tomato sauce
1 tablespoon oil
1 tablespoon wholemeal
   flour
¼ pint (125ml) water
8 oz (250g) tomatoes, peeled
   and chopped
½ teaspoon dried basil
1 tablespoon Parmesan
   cheese

American
6 ounces wholewheat pastry
2×3½ ounce cans sardines
   in tomato sauce
1 tablespoon oil
1 tablespoon wholewheat
   flour
⅔ cup water
8 ounces tomatoes, peeled
   and chopped
½ teaspoon dried basil
1 tablespoon Parmesan
   cheese

1. Use the pastry to line an 8 inch (20cm) flan tin. Arrange the sardines in the base.

2. Fry the onion in the oil for 5 minutes. Add the flour and cook for 2 minutes. Gradually stir in the water, then add the tomatoes and herbs. Cook for 10-15 minutes until the sauce is thick.

3. Pour the sauce over the sardines, sprinkle over the cheese, and bake at 400°F/200°C (Gas Mark 6) for 30 minutes. Serve hot or cold.

Fish Crumble (serves 4) 2

Imperial (Metric)	American
1 lb (500g) white fish	1 pound white fish
½ pint (250ml) milk	1¼ cups milk
4 oz (100g) prawns (optional)	4 ounces prawns (optional)
1 tablespoon vegetable margarine	1 tablespoon vegetable margarine
1 tablespoon wholemeal flour	1 tablespoon wholewheat flour
2 hard-boiled eggs	2 hard-boiled eggs
2 oz (50g) cooked peas	½ cup cooked peas

For the topping:

Imperial (Metric)	American
3 oz (75g) wholemeal flour	¾ cup wholewheat flour
1½ oz (37g) vegetable margarine	3 tablespoons vegetable margarine
2 oz (50g) grated cheese	½ cup grated cheese

1. Put the fish in an ovenproof dish with the milk and cook over a low heat, or bake in the oven at 350°F/180°C (Gas Mark 4), for about 20 minutes or until cooked through.

2. Drain off the milk and use to make a sauce with the margarine and the flour. Stir in the fish, prawns (if used), chopped eggs and peas. Put in an ovenproof dish.

3. To make the crumble rub the fat into the flour and stir in the cheese. Sprinkle over the fish and bake at 350°F/180°C (Gas Mark 4) for 30 minutes.

Desserts

The easiest and most nutritious dessert is fresh fruit, but if your family is anything like mine, they will demand something more for at least one meal of the day. The following recipes are almost all based on fresh or dried fruits.

Fresh Fruit Purée (serves 4) V2

Imperial (Metric)
2 bananas, sliced
1 eating apple, cored and
  chopped
2 oz (50g) dates
¼ pint (125ml) apple juice

American
2 bananas, sliced
1 eating apple, cored and
  chopped
½ cup dates
⅔ cup apple juice

1.   Put all the ingredients in a liquidizer and blend until smooth.

2.   Serve at once to prevent discolouration.

Apricot Fool (serves 4) V2

Imperial (Metric)
8 oz (250g) dried apricots,
   soaked overnight
¼ pint (125ml) natural
   yogurt
1 teaspoon clear honey
2 tablespoons dried milk
   powder

American
1½ cups dried apricots,
   soaked overnight
⅔ cup plain yogurt
1 teaspoon clear honey
2 tablespoons dried milk
   powder

1. Cook the apricots in the soaking water for about 15 minutes,
    until tender.

2. Drain, and put in a liquidizer with the other ingredients. Blend
    until smooth, adding a little of the cooking liquid or some
    orange juice, if necessary. If it tastes too sharp, add a little more
    honey.

3. Chill before serving.

Baked Orange Custards (serves 4) V2

Imperial (Metric)
⅓ pint (200ml) orange juice
2 eggs, beaten
2 teaspoons clear honey
1 orange, peeled and
   segmented

American
¾ cup orange juice
2 eggs, beaten
2 teaspoons clear honey
1 orange, peeled and
   segmented

1. Mix together the juice, eggs and honey. Pour into four lightly
    greased ramekin dishes, and bake in the oven at 300°F/150°C
    (Gas Mark 2) for about 30 minutes or until set.

2. To serve, turn out onto plates or bowls, and decorate with
    the orange segments.

Apple Crumble Pie (serves 4-6) V2

Imperial (Metric)
6 oz (150g) wholemeal pastry
1 lb (500g) cooking apples
2 tablespoons clear honey
2 oz (50g) raisins or sultanas
3 oz (75g) wholemeal flour
2 oz (50g) Muscovado sugar
3 oz (75g) vegetable
  margarine

American
6 ounces wholewheat pastry
1 pound cooking apples
2 tablespoons clear honey
⅓ cup dark or golden
  seedless raisins
¾ cup wholewheat flour
⅓ cup Muscovado sugar
⅓ cup vegetable margarine

1. Line an 8 inch (20cm) flan tin with the pastry. Peel, core and slice the apples, mix with the honey and raisins and put into the flan.

2. Make the crumble topping by mixing the flour and sugar, and rubbing in the margarine. Spread over the apple mixture.

3. Bake at 400°F/200°C (Gas Mark 6), for about 40 minutes or until the apple is cooked and the top is golden-brown. Serve hot or cold.

Banana and Date Pudding (serves 4) V2

Imperial (Metric)
3 oz (75g) vegetable
  margarine
3 oz (75g) raw cane sugar
1 egg, beaten
4 oz (100g) self-raising
  wholemeal flour
2 oz (50g) dates, chopped
2 tablespoons milk
1 lb (500g) bananas, sliced

American
⅓ cup vegetable margarine
½ cup raw cane sugar
1 egg, beaten
1 cup self-raising
  wholewheat flour
⅓ cup dates, chopped
2 tablespoons milk
1 pound bananas, sliced

1. Cream the margarine and sugar, and beat in the egg. Fold in
    the flour, dates and milk.

2. Put the sliced bananas in an 8 inch (20cm) China flan dish,
    and spoon the pudding over. Bake at 375°F/190°C (Gas Mark
    5) for about 35 minutes, until risen and golden. Serve hot
    or cold.

Rhubarb Meringue (serves 4) V2

Imperial (Metric)
1 lb (500g) rhubarb
Rind and juice of 1 orange
1 oz (25g) raw cane sugar
2 oz (50g) fresh wholemeal
  bread or cake crumbs
2 egg yolks

American
1 pound rhubarb
Rind and juice of 1 orange
2 tablespoons raw cane sugar
1 cup fresh wholewheat
  bread or cake crumbs
2 egg yolks

For the topping:

Imperial (Metric)
3 egg whites
2 oz (50g) raw cane sugar
2 oz (50g) ground almonds
3 tablespoons flaked
  almonds

American
3 egg whites
¼ cup raw cane sugar
¼ cup ground almonds
3 tablespoons slivered
  almonds

1. Chop the rhubarb into even-sized pieces and cook for 5 minutes with the orange juice, rind and sugar.

2. Lift out the fruit with a slotted spoon, mix in the bread or cake crumbs and the egg yolks, and put into an ovenproof dish. Cook in the oven at 350°F/180°C (Gas Mark 4) for 15 minutes or until set.

3. Beat the egg whites until stiff but not dry. Fold in the sugar and ground almonds with a metal spoon. Spoon over the rhubarb. Sprinkle almonds over. Bake at 400°F/200°C (Gas Mark 6) for 20-30 minutes. Serve hot or cold.

Banana and Honey Flapjack (serves 4) V

Imperial (Metric)
3 tablespoons clear honey
2 oz (50g) vegetable
   margarine
4 oz (100g) muesli
1 lb (500g) bananas, sliced

American
3 tablespoons clear honey
¼ cup vegetable margarine
1 cup muesli
1 pound bananas, sliced

1. Melt the honey and margarine over a low heat and stir in the muesli.

2. Put the sliced bananas in a shallow heatproof dish. Spoon the flapjack topping over. Cook under a preheated grill (broiler) at medium heat until top is golden all over. Watch carefully as it burns easily.

Home-made Jelly (Jello) (serves 4) 2

This does not take more than a few minutes to make, and is certainly much more nutritious than the bought varieties, which are full of sugar, flavourings and colourings. The addition of the fruit purée adds considerably to the flavour, but is not essential. You can also add chopped fresh fruit.

Imperial (Metric)
1 pint (500ml) fruit juice
1 tablespoon gelatine
2 tablespoons clear honey
¼ pint (125ml) fruit purée
   (optional)

American
2½ cups fruit juice
1 tablespoon gelatine
2 tablespoons clear honey
⅔ cup fruit purée (optional)

1. Reserve 2 tablespoons of juice, and heat the rest to boiling point.

2. Stir the gelatine into the 2 tablespoons of juice, and leave to stand for a few minutes.

3. As soon as the juice reaches boiling point, remove from the heat and stir in the gelatine mixture.

4. Continue to stir for a few minutes until the gelatine is thoroughly dissolved, ie., no more granules are visible.

5. Stir in the fruit purée or fresh fruit if used, pour into a bowl or jelly (jello) mould, and chill until set.

Brown Rice Pudding (serves 4) V2

Imperial (Metric)	American
1 pint (500ml) milk	*2½ cups milk*
4 oz (100g) short grain brown rice	*½ cup shortgrain brown rice*
2 tablespoons raw cane sugar (optional)	*2 tablespoons raw cane sugar (optional)*
1 egg, beaten	*1 egg, beaten*
Good pinch of freshly grated nutmeg	*Good pinch of freshly grated nutmeg*
4 oz (100g) mixed dried fruit, soaked overnight, drained and chopped (optional)	*½ cup mixed dried fruit, soaked overnight, drained and chopped (optional)*

1. Bring the milk to the boil, stir in the rice, cover and simmer gently for 45 minutes. Keep an eye on it to make sure it does not boil over.

2. Remove from the heat and stir in the sugar (if used), the egg and the grated nutmeg.

3. Put layers of the rice and dried fruit (if used) in a greased ovenproof dish, finishing with the rice. Bake at 350°F/180°C (Gas Mark 4) for 30 minutes.

For a baby:
Omit the nutmeg.

Home-made Ice-cream

I am including two recipes for ice-cream (which seems to be a staple item in the diet of many children), and you may like to try both since they each have a distinctive taste. The first one is richer than the second, as it is based on cream rather than evaporated milk. Both have the advantages of being quick and easy to make, low in sugar, and made from wholesome ingredients, unlike the bought varieties which usually have sugar high on the ingredients list, and contain flavouring and colouring. The cream used in the first recipe is whipping cream, as this has considerably less fat than double (heavy) cream — 35-42 per cent, compared with 48-60 per cent in the latter. Both the recipes can have other flavours added. For instance, try adding 2 ounces (50g) melted carob, or 2 ounces (50g) chopped nuts, or 4 ounces (100g) chopped fresh fruit or ¼ pint (125ml/⅔ cup) fruit purée.

Vanilla Ice-cream 1 (makes about 2 pints/ 1 litre/5 cups) V2

Imperial (Metric)
2 eggs, separated
1 oz (25g) raw cane sugar
¼ pint (125ml) whipping cream
1 teaspoon natural vanilla essence

American
2 eggs, separated
2 tablespoons raw cane sugar
⅔ cup whipping cream
1 teaspoon natural vanilla essence

1. Beat the egg whites until stiff, but not dry, and beat in the sugar.

2. Beat the egg yolks and gradually add to the whites, together with the vanilla essence.

3. Lightly whip the cream and fold into the whites with a metal spoon. Pour into a lidded plastic container and freeze until set. Place in the fridge 30 minutes before serving.

Vanilla Ice-cream II (makes about 2 pints/ 1 litre/5 cups) 2

Imperial (Metric)

1×14 oz (400g) tin
  evaporated milk
2 tablespoons raw cane sugar
1 teaspoon gelatine
2 tablespoons water
1 egg, beaten
1 teaspoon natural vanilla
  essence

American

1×14 ounce can evaporated
  milk
2 tablespoons raw cane sugar
1 teaspoon gelatine
2 tablespoons water
1 egg, beaten
1 teaspoon natural vanilla
  essence

1. Chill the evaporated milk for 1 hour.

2. Mix the sugar, gelatine and water in a cup and dissolve by standing the cup in a pan of simmering water.

3. Whip the milk until light and frothy, and gradually beat in the other ingredients. Pour into a lidded plastic container and freeze until set. Remove from the freezer 15 minutes before serving.

Note: This ice-cream sometimes separates out slightly on freezing, but this can be avoided by removing the ice-cream from the freezer when it is half set and beating it again before returning it to the freezer.

Breads, Biscuits and Cakes

As explained in other parts of this book, eating between meals is to be discouraged, especially when it involves sweet foods. However, there are times when it is nice to offer home-made cakes and biscuits; for instance, on special occasions, as part of a packed lunch, or to round off a snack meal. If you bake your own, you have the advantage of knowing just what has gone into them, you can use the best ingredients without any need for artificial flavourings, colourings or preservatives, and you can choose low-sugar recipes. Those included here fulfil these criteria.

Baking at home often works out considerably cheaper (for instance, in the case of bread), and if you own a freezer you can save time and money by batch baking.

No-Knead Wholemeal Bread (makes 3 loaves) V2

Imperial (Metric)	American
1 oz (25g) fresh yeast or ½ oz (13g) dried yeast	2½ tablespoons fresh yeast or 1 tablespoon dried yeast
2 teaspoons raw cane sugar	2 teaspoons raw cane sugar
2 teaspoons margarine	2 teaspoons margarine
3 lb (1.5 kilos) wholemeal flour	12 cups wholewheat flour
2 teaspoons sea salt	2 teaspoons sea salt
1½ pints (750ml) warm (110°F/43°C) water (approx.)	3¾ cups warm (110°F/43°C) water (approx.)

1. Mix the yeast, sugar, margarine and ¼ pint (125ml/⅔ cup) of the water and leave in a warm place for about 10 minutes until frothy.

2. Mix the flour and salt and add the yeast liquid, together with the rest of the water. Add the water gradually towards the end as different flours will require different amounts of liquid — you are aiming for a soft but not sticky dough.

3. Divide the dough into three and place in warm, greased tins. Cover and leave to rise in a warm place for about 30 minutes. Meanwhile, preheat the oven to 425°F/220°C (Gas Mark 7). Bake the loaves for 35 minutes. Cool on a wire tray.

To vary:
Add 2 tablespoons sesame seeds or cracked wheat, or 6 tablespoons soya flour.

You can also use this basic recipe to make bread rolls, in which case shape them into rounds, place on a warm, greased baking sheet and leave in a warm place to rise for 15 minutes, before baking for 15 minutes.

Wholemeal Pitta Bread (makes 8) V2

Imperial (Metric)	American
½ oz (13g) fresh yeast	1¼ tablespoons fresh yeast
½ pint (250ml) warm water (110°F/43°C)	1¼ cups warm water (110°F/43°C)
1 teaspoon raw cane sugar	1 teaspoon raw cane sugar
1 lb (500g) wholemeal flour	4 cups wholewheat flour
1 teaspoon sea salt	1 teaspoon sea salt
2 teaspoons oil	2 teaspoons oil

1. Mix the yeast, water and sugar. Add the flour and salt and knead for 5 minutes. Add the oil and knead again for 5 minutes. Place the dough in an oiled bowl and cover with an oiled plastic bag. Leave to rise in a warm place for about 2 hours.

2. Weigh out eight equal portions, knead into balls and flatten to ¼ inch (5mm) thick. Place on a flat floured surface, cover with a cloth, and leave to rise again for about 20 minutes.

3. Meanwhile grease and warm two baking sheets, and preheat the oven to 450°F/230°C (Gas Mark 8). Carefully put the pitta on to the trays, brush with water, and bake for 10 minutes near the top of the oven until light and puffy. Cover with a cloth and cool on a wire rack. To serve, split and fill with desired stuffing, e.g., grated cheese, chopped raw vegetables, cooked pulses.

Barley Bannocks (makes 8) V2

Imperial (Metric)
6 oz (150g) self-raising
   wholemeal flour
4 oz (100g) barley flour
1 teaspoon sea salt
1 level teaspoon bicarbonate
   of soda
½ level teaspoon cream of
   tartar
1 oz (25g) vegetable
   margarine
⅓ pint (200ml) milk
   (approx.)

American
1½ cups self-raising
   wholewheat flour
½ cup barley flour
1 teaspoon sea salt
1 level teaspoon baking soda
½ level teaspoon cream of
   tartar
2½ tablespoons vegetable
   margarine
¾ cup milk (approx.)

1. Preheat the oven to 400°F/200°C (Gas Mark 6).

2. Mix together all the dry ingredients. Rub in the margarine, and add enough milk to give a soft but not sticky dough.

3. On a floured surface pat or roll out to a circle about ½ inch (1cm) thick, and cut into 8 portions. Place on a greased baking tray and bake for about 12 minutes.

To vary:
Replace the barley flour with oatmeal.

Basic Wholemeal Pastry (for one 8-9 inch/20-30cm flan) V2

Imperial (Metric)	American
6 oz (150g) wholemeal flour	1½ cups wholewheat flour
3 oz (75g) soft vegetable margarine	⅓ cup soft vegetable margarine
1½ tablespoons cold water (approx.)	1½ tablespoons cold water (approx.)

1. Put the flour in a bowl and rub in the margarine until the mixture resembles fine breadcrumbs. Add the water a little at a time, adding just enough to bind the mixture together without making it sticky. (Wholemeal flour tends to absorb more water than white flour.)

2. On a floured surface roll out the pastry, rolling in each direction without attempting to turn the pastry. When the correct size is obtained, loosen the pastry from the rolling surface with a palette knife. Lift carefully into the flan tin by draping over the rolling pin. (Wholemeal pastry is more difficult to manoeuvre than white but, providing it is forming the base of a pie you can always patch it back together again if it should tear, and no one will be any the wiser.)

3. To give a nice crisp pastry for a flan, prick the pastry all over with a fork and bake at 425°F/220°C (Gas Mark 7) for 5-10 minutes before adding the filling.

Applejacks (makes about 20)

For the filling:

Imperial (Metric)	American
1 lb (500g) cooking apples	1 pound cooking apples
2 oz (50g) butter	¼ cup butter
2 oz (50g) raw cane sugar	⅓ cup raw cane sugar
2 oz (50g) raisins	⅓ cup raisins

For the flapjacks:

Imperial (Metric)	American
7 tablespoons runny honey	7 tablespoons runny honey
6 oz (150g) margarine	¾ cup margarine
4 oz (100g) raw cane sugar	⅔ cup raw cane sugar
1 lb (500g) porridge oats	4 cups porridge oats
1 oz (25g) sesame seeds	¼ cup sesame seeds
1 oz (25g) sunflower seeds	¼ cup sunflower seeds

1. Peel, core and slice the apples. Cook with the butter over a low heat for about 10 minutes, or until soft. Remove from the heat and beat with a wooden spoon. Add sugar and cook for a further 10 minutes until mixture thickens. Add raisins and leave to cool.

2. Melt honey and margarine together and stir in sugar, oats, and seeds. Grease an 11×7 inch (27×18cm) tin and press in half the flapjack mixture. Spread over the apple filling, and then scatter over the rest of the oat mixture, smoothing the surface with the back of a wetted spoon.

3. Bake at 350°F/180°C (Gas Mark 4) for 50 minutes, until firm and golden. Cool in the tin and then cut into squares. Can also be served warm as a dessert. This freezes well.

Sesame Snaps (makes about 24) V

Imperial (Metric)
6 oz (150g) vegetable
  margarine
1 tablespoon honey
3 oz (75g) raw cane sugar
4 oz (100g) wholemeal flour
6 oz (150g) porridge oats
2 oz (50g) toasted sesame
  seeds

American
¾ cup vegetable margarine
1 tablespoon honey
½ cup raw cane sugar
1 cup wholewheat flour
1½ cups rolled oats
⅓ cup toasted sesame seeds

1. Melt the margarine, honey and sugar. Mix together all the
    ingredients and press into a greased 13×9 inch (33×23cm)
    tin. Bake at 325°F/170°C (Gas Mark 3) for 30 minutes or until
    golden. Cut into squares, and leave in the tin until cold.

Fruit Bars (makes about 24) V

Imperial (Metric)
4 oz (100g) dates, stoned
4 oz (100g) dried apricots
4 oz (100g) dried figs
2 oz (50g) raisins
1 tablespoon sesame seeds
4 oz (100g) mixed nuts

American
1 cup dates, stoned
1 cup dried apricots
1 cup dried figs
⅓ cup raisins
1 tablespoon sesame seeds
¾ cup mixed nuts

1. Finely mince all the ingredients and mix thoroughly. Press
    into a greased 11×7 inch (27×18cm) tin and leave to harden
    for a few hours before cutting into bars.

Wholemeal Scones (makes about 12)

Imperial (Metric)
8 oz (250g) wholemeal flour
1 teaspoon baking powder
½ teaspoon sea salt
2 oz (50g) vegetable
  margarine
1 tablespoon raw cane sugar
¼ pint (125ml) natural
  yogurt
Milk and sesame seeds to
  coat

American
2 cups wholewheat flour
1 teaspoon baking powder
½ teaspoon sea salt
¼ cup vegetable margarine
1 tablespoon raw cane sugar
⅔ cup plain yogurt
Milk and sesame seeds to
  coat

1. Preheat the oven to 425°F/220°C (Gas Mark 7). Mix together the dry ingredients. Rub in the margarine until the mixture resembles fine breadcrumbs. Stir in the sugar, add the yogurt and mix to a soft dough.

2. Knead lightly on a floured surface and roll out to ¾ inch (2cm) thick. Cut into 2 inch (5cm) rounds or into triangles and place on a greased and floured baking sheet.

3. Brush with milk, sprinkle with sesame seeds, and bake for 12-15 minutes. Cool on a wire rack.

For a baby:
Omit the sesame seeds.

Digestive Biscuits (Graham Crackers)
(makes about 24) V2

Imperial (Metric)	American
8 oz (250g) wholemeal flour	2 cups wholewheat flour
Pinch sea salt	Pinch sea salt
1 teaspoon baking powder	1 teaspoon baking powder
3 oz (75g) margarine	⅓ cup margarine
1 oz (25g) raw cane sugar	1 tablespoon raw cane sugar
1 small egg, beaten	1 small egg, beaten
2 tablespoons milk	2 tablespoons milk
1 tablespoon sesame seeds	1 tablespoon sesame seeds

1. Heat the oven to 375°F/190°C (Gas Mark 5). Mix the dry ingredients and rub in the margarine until the mixture resembles fine breadcrumbs.

2. Add the rest of the ingredients and mix well to a firm dough.

3. On a floured surface roll out thinly and cut into 2½ inch (6cm) rounds.

4. Place on a greased baking sheet and prick all over with a fork. Brush with water and sprinkle with sesame seeds. Bake for 15-20 minutes. Cool on a wire rack.

For a baby:
Omit the sesame seeds.

Apricot Bars (makes 25-30) V

For the base:

Imperial (Metric)	American
4 oz (100g) vegetable margarine	⅔ cup vegetable margarine
8 oz (250g) wholemeal flour	2 cups wholewheat flour
2 oz (50g) raw cane sugar	⅓ cup raw cane sugar

For the top:

Imperial (Metric)	American
8 oz (250g) dried apricots, soaked overnight	2 cups dried apricots, soaked overnight
2 eggs	2 eggs
3 oz (75g) raw cane sugar	½ cup raw cane sugar
4 oz (100g) wholemeal flour	1 cup wholewheat flour
½ teaspoon natural vanilla essence	½ teaspoon natural vanilla essence
2 oz (50g) chopped walnuts	½ cup chopped English walnuts

1. Rub the margarine into the flour until mixture resembles fine breadcrumbs. Add the sugar and knead together. Press mixture into a flat baking tray approx. 10 × 12inches (25 × 30cm). Bake for 15 minutes at 350°F/180°C (Gas Mark 4).

2. Meanwhile simmer the apricots in their soaking water for 10 minutes. Drain and chop.

3. Beat the eggs and sugar together until pale and frothy, and mix in the other topping ingredients. Spread over the base and bake for a further 30 minutes. Cut into squares, but leave in the tin until cold.

Oat and Nut Biscuits (makes 35) V2

Imperial (Metric)
6 oz (150g) vegetable
  margarine
3 oz (75g) raw cane sugar
1 egg, beaten
8 oz (250g) wholemeal flour
2 oz (50g) ground almonds
½ teaspoon natural almond
  essence

American
¾ cup vegetable margarine
½ cup raw cane sugar
1 egg, beaten
2 cups wholewheat plain
  flour
½ cup ground almonds
½ teaspoon natural almond
  essence

To coat:

Imperial (Metric)
1-2 oz (25-50g) porridge oats
Chopped or whole nuts

American
¼ - ½ cup rolled oats
Chopped or whole nuts

1. Mix together all the biscuit ingredients to form a soft dough.
   Weigh out ½ oz (13g) pieces and roll into balls.

2. Dip in the oats, put on a greased baking tray, and press flat
   with the back of a fork.

3. Place a nut in the centre of each biscuit, and bake at
   350°F/180°C (Gas Mark 4) for 25 minutes. Cool on a wire rack.

For a baby:
Omit the nut on top.

Banana and Date Cake V2

Imperial (Metric)	American
5 oz (125g) vegetable margarine	½ cup vegetable margarine
2 oz (50g) raw cane sugar	⅓ cup raw cane sugar
1 egg, beaten	1 egg, beaten
5 oz (125g) mashed banana	5 ounces mashed banana
2 tablespoons runny honey	2 tablespoons runny honey
6 oz (150g) chopped dates	1 cup chopped dates
10 oz (300g) wholemeal self-raising flour	2½ cups wholewheat self-raising flour

1. Heat the oven to 325°F/170°C (Gas Mark 3). Cream the margarine and sugar until light and fluffy. Beat in the egg. Stir in the rest of the ingredients and mix well. Put into a greased 8½ inch (22cm) cake tin and bake in the centre of the oven for about 1¼ hours, or until cake feels firm. Cool on a wire rack.

Fruity Malt Bread (makes 2 small loaves or 1 large) V2

Imperial (Metric)	American
1 oz (25g) vegetable margarine	2½ tablespoons vegetable margarine
1 lb (500g) wholemeal flour	2 cups wholewheat flour
1½ teaspoons baking powder	1½ teaspoons baking powder
½ level teaspoon sea salt	½ level teaspoon sea salt
1 tablespoon runny honey	1 tablespoon runny honey
1 tablespoon molasses	1 tablespoon molasses
½ pint (250ml) milk	1¼ cups milk
4 oz (100g) raisins or sultanas	⅔ cup dark or golden seedless raisins
2 heaped tablespoons malt extract	2 heaped tablespoons malt extract

1. Heat the oven to 325°F/170°C (Gas Mark 3). Grease and line 2 small or 1 large loaf tin.

2. Mix together the dry ingredients and rub in the margarine. Gently heat together the milk, honey, molasses and malt.

3. Add to the flour together with the raisins, and beat well for 1 minute. Put into the tin or tins and bake in the centre of the oven for about 1 hour for the small loaves or about 1 hour 20 minutes for the large loaf.

Note: If liked the loaves can be brushed with a glaze as soon as they are removed from the oven. To prepare a glaze mix together 1 tablespoon each of water, milk and sugar. Bring to the boil and remove from the heat.

DRINKS

Your baby's first drinks (other than milk) can be given when he is only a few weeks old, and it is up to you whether you choose to give him plain boiled water or something more nutritious. The important thing at this as at later stages is to steer clear of sugar-laden drinks like squashes.

Fresh orange juice is a good one to start with since it is a rich source of vitamin C. It must be diluted at first, adding a tablespoon of boiled water to a teaspoon of strained juice. Give this for two or three days in between feeds but only if the baby is awake, since it is by no means essential. If there are no ill effects, such as a rash, vomiting or diarrhoea, you can increase the proportion of juice to two teaspoons, gradually working up to equal quantities of juice and water. Babies often prefer a drink at room temperature or slightly warm (breastfed babies are used to warm fluids!), but do not make it too hot or you will destroy some of the vitamin C content.

If your baby does show a reaction to orange juice, tomato juice is often an acceptable alternative, and one which also provides vitamin C.

At this age your baby can take his drink from a spoon or a bottle, but by the time he is four or five months old he should be able to manage a spouted beaker, or even a cup if you do not mind coping with the inevitable spillages.

Milk

Once your baby is weaned there is no need to force him to drink lots of cow's milk, provided his diet contains other calcium-rich sources, such as leafy green vegetables, sesame seeds, molasses, pulses (especially soya), carob, oily fish and dried fruit, especially figs, apricots and dates. Although great emphasis is placed on milk as a nutritious food for babies and children, a growing number of authorities consider milk to be totally unsuitable for human consumption. After all, it was intended for calves, not people!

Milk certainly provides nothing which is not easily obtained elsewhere in the diet, and dairy fat, as a saturated fat, is one of those implicated in heart disease. Milk is also mucus-forming, and it is advisable to cut out both this and other dairy produce at the first signs of a cold, or permanently if your child is prone to colds, ear infections, respiratory problems or catarrhal complaints. Milk is also one of the most common causes of allergy among children — as much as 92 per cent of cases according to one source.

If your child does not like milk to drink there is, as you can see, no cause for concern. None of my three children has ever drunk milk and it has certainly done them no harm. It is at any rate possible to incorporate a fair amount of milk in cooking, such as in sauces, milk puddings and egg custards, or to serve it with breakfast cereals. The best types to use are skimmed or semi-skimmed since these are lower in fat. And if your child eats cheese he will be getting all the calcium he needs without any trouble, since it contains almost seven times as much as milk. Yogurt is another calcium-rich food that is often popular even with those who dislike the milk from which it is made.

There are a number of alternatives to milk which can be served after weaning. Goat's milk, for instance, is digested more quickly, easily and completely than cow's milk, since the fat globules are much smaller. It is not mucus-forming, is 50 per cent higher in vitamin B_1, and is also rich in vitamin A, calcium and phosphorus. Another plus point for goat's milk is that it is less likely to cause an allergic reaction. Indeed, one survey involving 300 children who suffered from asthma due to cow's milk allergy, found that 270 were free from symptoms after six weeks on goat's milk. It depends whether the allergy is to the lactalbumin in cow's milk or the casein. If it is the latter (which is much more unlikely) then the child may be allergic to goat's milk as well.

A growing number of health food shops and supermarkets are now stocking goat's milk, usually frozen in cartons or plastic sachets, but it is worth shopping around since prices vary considerably. Some people find goat's milk unpalatable, but if it is fresh it should not have a strong flavour. If your child dislikes the taste, you can still serve it undetected in cooking. Goat's milk is also available in dried powder, but this works out considerably more expensive.

Soya milk, which can be made at home or purchased in tins, cartons or powdered form, is rich in protein, will not cause allergies, and is easy to digest. It even comes in flavoured varieties and it is now possible to buy brands which do not contain added sugar.

Nut or seed milks are easy to make at home, and have a delicious flavour which can be varied according to the type of nut or seed used. See page 170 for the recipe.

Choosing a daily drink

As your baby gets older, you will need to decide what he is going to drink on a regular basis. Tea and coffee are of course even less suitable for children than they are for adults, and orange squash and other sugary drinks, whether fizzy or still, are not to be recommended.

In fact, although people commonly use the term 'squash', this product is very difficult to obtain these days, since it has been almost universally replaced by orange drink. Most people are not even aware of this change (needless to say, the manufacturers have not advertized it), but there is a substantial difference, in that the drink may contain up to 40 per cent less fruit than the squash.

This means that orange squash (if you can find it) must have 25 per cent pure juice, whereas orange drink need contain only 10 per cent comminuted orange (i.e., minced fruit including peel, pith and pips). Orange nectar is 50 per cent juice; barley water is 15 per cent plus barley flour; and orange crush is 5 per cent juice when ready to drink. Orangeade and other fizzy fruit drinks contain little or no fruit, being more likely to rely on flavourings. A cordial is a clear squash or crush.

A product termed 'pure juice' is 100 per cent but mostly reconstituted, a fact which is revealed by the words 'made from concentrated orange juice'. The orange juice is concentrated by evaporation and is then frozen and shipped to this country, where it is rediluted and flash pasteurized before packing. Pure orange juice which is not reconstituted is difficult to find, and is much more expensive. When buying juice go for frozen, canned or cartonned, in preference to glass bottles where the juice has considerably less vitamin C. Pasteurization and storage both reduce a juice's vitamin C content, and in this respect the best kind of juice to serve is your own, freshly squeezed just before drinking.

If your child is used to drinking fresh juice from an early age, then squash will seem excessively sweet. Juice certainly works out more expensive than squash, but if you can continue to give it to your child as he gets older you at least have the reassurance that it is doing him good. And it can be served very diluted, or the number of drinks restricted, with water being offered instead.

You can also make up your own drinks at home, using recipes like those that follow. Most of these are quick and easy to prepare, although they do call for a blender. The following will give you some ideas, but in fact the combinations are endless.

Carob Milk (makes ¼ pint/125ml/⅔ cup)

Imperial (Metric)	American
¼ pint (125ml) milk	⅔ cup milk
1-2 teaspoons carob powder	1-2 teaspoons carob powder

1. Whisk the two together and serve immediately, or chill and stir before serving.

Fruit Cocktail (makes about ⅓ pint/200ml/¾ cup)

Imperial (Metric)
1 slice fresh pineapple or 2
  slices tinned pineapple
¼ pint (125ml) orange juice
½ banana, sliced

American
1 slice fresh pineapple or 2
  slices canned pineapple
⅔ cup orange juice
½ banana, sliced

1.   Put all the ingredients in a liquidizer and blend until smooth.

2.   Strain through a sieve.

To vary:
Use other fruits and/or add any of the following: honey, yogurt, cottage or cream cheese. For instance, ¼ pint (125ml/⅔ cup) pineapple juice with 1 tablespoon cottage cheese — makes ¼ pint (125ml/⅔ cup); ¼ pint (125ml/⅔ cup) orange juice with 1 tablespoon cream cheese — makes ¼ pint (125ml/⅔ cup); ¼ pint (125ml/⅔ cup) apple juice with ¼ pint (125ml/⅔ cup) natural yogurt — makes about ½ pint (250ml/1¼ cups).

Nut or Seed Milk
(makes about 2 pints/1 litre/5 cups)

Imperial (Metric)
4 oz (100g) nuts or seeds
2 pints (1 litre) water

American
1 cup nuts or seeds
5 cups water

1.   Soak the nuts or seeds in the water overnight.

2.   Blend until smooth. Pour through a fine sieve. Chill.

To vary:
Try a variety of different nuts and seeds — almonds and cashews are particularly popular with my family.

Banana Milk (makes about ⅓ pint/200ml/¾ cup)

Imperial (Metric)
¼ pint (125ml) milk
1 whole egg or 1 egg yolk
1 banana, sliced
1 teaspoon runny honey
1 teaspoon wheatgerm

American
⅔ cup milk
1 whole egg or 1 egg yolk
1 banana, sliced
1 teaspoon runny honey
1 teaspoon wheatgerm

1. Put all the ingredients into a liquidizer and blend until smooth.

2. Strain through a sieve and serve immediately.

To vary:
Substitute other fruit, and/or omit the egg.

Orange Yogurt Drink (makes ¾ pint/375ml/2 cups)

Imperial (Metric)
¼ pint (125ml) natural
  yogurt
1 egg
¼ pint (125ml) orange juice
2 teaspoons runny honey

American
⅔ cup plain yogurt
1 egg
⅔ cup orange juice
2 teaspoons runny honey

1. Put all the ingredients in a liquidizer and blend until smooth.

Apple Juice (makes ½ pint/250ml/1¼ cups)

Imperial (Metric)
2 eating apples
½ pint (250ml) boiling water

American
2 eating apples
1¼ cups boiling water

1. Core and chop the apples and simmer in the water in a tightly
    covered pan for 15 minutes. Cool and strain.

Fresh Fruit Juices
(makes about ⅓ pint/200ml/¾ cup)

Imperial (Metric)
6 oz (150g) fresh fruit,
   chopped
¼ pint (125ml) water

American
1 cup chopped fresh fruit
⅔ cup water

1. Place ingredients in a liquidizer and blend until smooth.

2. Strain through a piece of muslin.

Buttermilk Fruit Drink
(makes ¾ pint/375ml/2 cups)

Imperial (Metric)
½ pint (250ml) buttermilk
1 orange, peeled and
   chopped
1 tablespoon runny honey
Juice of ½ lemon

American
1¼ cups buttermilk
1 orange, peeled and
   chopped
1 tablespoon runny honey
Juice of ½ lemon

1. Place all the ingredients in a liquidizer and blend until smooth.
   Strain.

Appleade (makes ¼ pint/125ml/⅔ cup)

Imperial (Metric)
¼ pint (125ml) apple juice
2 tablespoons lemon juice
2 teaspoons runny honey
4 oz (100g) grated apple

American
⅔ cup apple juice
2 tablespoons lemon juice
2 teaspoons runny honey
⅔ cup grated apple

1. Put all the ingredients in a liquidizer and blend until smooth.
   Strain.

Lemonade
(makes about 1½ pints/750ml/3¾ cups)

Imperial (Metric)
3 lemons
1½ pints (750ml) boiling
  water
3-4 oz (75-100g) Demerara
  sugar

American
3 lemons
3¾ cups boiling water
½-⅔ cup Demerara sugar

1. Thinly peel the rind from 1½ lemons and put in a large basin. Pour on the boiling water and add the sugar, stirring until dissolved. Cover and leave until cool.

2. Add the lemon juice, strain and chill before serving.

To vary:
Make orangeade by using 2 oranges and 1 lemon, and about 2 oz (50g/⅓ cup) sugar.

Lemon Barley Water
(makes 1 pint/500ml/2½ cups)

Imperial (Metric)
2 oz (50g) pot barley
1 pint (500ml) boiling water
2 lemons
2 oz (50g) Demerara sugar

American
¼ cup pot barley
2½ cups boiling water
2 lemons
⅓ cup Demerara sugar

1. Add the barley and the thinly peeled rind of 1 lemon to the boiling water. Simmer gently for ½ hour, remove from heat and stir in the sugar and the lemon juice. Leave to cool.

2. Strain and taste, adding extra sugar if necessary. Chill before serving.

Mixed Vegetable Juice
(makes ⅔ pint/350ml/1½ cups)

Imperial (Metric)	American
2 carrots, sliced	2 carrots, sliced
3 sticks celery, chopped	3 stalks celery, chopped
1 eating apple, cored and chopped	1 eating apple, cored and chopped
4 tomatoes, chopped	4 tomatoes, chopped
⅓ pint (200ml) water or tomato juice	¾ cup water or tomato juice

1.   Put all the ingredients in a liquidizer and blend until smooth.

2.   Strain through muslin and chill before serving.

To vary:
Use other vegetables, such as beetroot, watercress, or beansprouts.

Homemade Ice Lollies (drinks on sticks)
You can buy some excellent plastic containers for making your own lollies — much cheaper and more nutritious than bought lollies, which are full of sugar, colouring and flavouring. Try some of the following:

● fresh fruit juice
● equal parts of fruit juice and puréed fruit
● equal parts of fruit juice and yogurt
● 2 teaspoons carob powder stirred into ¼ pint (125ml/⅔ cup) milk
● yogurt with dried fruit and honey
● yogurt with fruit purée
● milk with grated apple

INDEX